1 Abide with me

1 Abide with me; fast falls the eventide;
   The darkness deepens; Lord, with me ~
   When other helpers fail, and comforts flee,
   Help of the helpless, O abide with me!

2 Swift to its close ebbs out life's little day;
   Earth's joys grow dim, its glories pass away;
   Change and decay in all around I see:
   O Thou who changest not, abide with me!

3 I need Thy presence ev'ry passing hour;
   What but Thy grace can foil the tempter's pow'r?
   Who like Thyself my guide and stay can be?
   Through cloud and sunshine, O abide with me!

4 I fear no foe, with Thee at hand to bless;
   Ills have no weight, and tears no bitterness;
   Where is death's sting? Where, grave, thy victory?
   I triumph still, if Thou abide with me.

5 Hold Thou Thy cross before my closing eyes,
   Shine through the gloom, and point me to the skies;
   Heav'n's morning breaks, and earth's vain shadows flee:
   In life, in death, O Lord, abide with me!

Henry Francis Lyte (1793–1847)

2 *Alleluia, alleluia, give thanks to the risen Lord*

Alleluia, alleluia, give thanks to the risen Lord,
Alleluia, alleluia, give praise to His name.

1 Jesus is Lord of all the earth.
   He is the King of creation.
   Alleluia . . .

2 Spread the good news o'er all the earth,
   Jesus has died and has risen.
   Alleluia . . .

3 We have been crucified with Christ,
   Now we shall live for ever.
   Alleluia . . .

4 God has proclaimed the just reward,
   Life for all men, alleluia.
   Alleluia . . .

5 Come let us praise the living God,
   Joyfully sing to our Saviour.
   Alleluia . . .

Don Fishel

3 All glory, laud and honour

1 All glory, laud and honour
   To Thee, Redeemer, King,
   To whom the lips of children
   Made sweet hosannas ring.
   Thou art the King of Israel,
   Thou David's royal Son,
   Who in the Lord's name comest,
   The King and blessèd one.

2 The company of angels
   Are praising Thee on high,
   And mortal men and all things
   Created make reply.
   The people of the Hebrews
   With psalms before Thee went;
   Our praise and prayer and anthems
   Before Thee we present.

3 To Thee before Thy passion
   They sang their hymns of praise;
   To Thee now high exalted
   Our melody we raise.
   Thou didst accept their praises;
   Accept the prayers we bring,
   Who in all good delightest,
   Thou good and gracious King.

Theodulph of Orleans (c750–821)
trans. J.M. Neale (1818–1866)

4 *All hail the power of Jesus' name*

MILES LANE

With vigour

All hail the pow'r of Je - sus'__name! Let an - gels__pros - trate
fall; Bring forth the roy - al di - a - dem, And crown Him,
crown Him, crown Him, Crown Him Lord of all.

Suggested accompaniment:
Brass instruments for the last six bars (crescendo).

4

1 All hail the pow'r of Jesus' name!
  Let angels prostrate fall;
  Bring forth the royal diadem,
  And crown Him, crown Him, crown Him,
  Crown Him Lord of all.

2 Crown Him, ye martyrs of our God,
  Who from His altar call;
  Extol the stem of Jesse's rod,
  And crown Him, crown Him, crown Him,
  Crown Him Lord of all.

3 Ye seed of Israel's chosen race,
  And ransomed from the fall,
  Hail Him who saves you by His grace,
  And crown Him, crown Him, crown Him,
  Crown Him Lord of all.

4 Let ev'ry kindred, ev'ry tribe
  On this terrestrial ball,
  To Him all majesty ascribe,
  And crown Him, crown Him, crown Him,
  Crown Him Lord of all.

5 O that with yonder sacred throng
  We at His feet may fall,
  Join in the everlasting song,
  And crown Him, crown Him, crown Him,
  Crown Him Lord of all!

Edward Perronet (1726–92),
John Rippon (1751–1836)

5

5 All over the world

1 All over the world the Spirit is moving,
  All over the world as the prophet said it would be;
  All over the world there's a mighty revelation
  Of the glory of the Lord, as the waters cover the sea.

2 Deep down in my heart the Spirit is moving,
  Deep down in my heart as the prophet said it would be;
  Deep down in my heart there's a mighty revelation
  Of the glory of the Lord, as the waters cover the sea.

author unknown

Joel 2: 28, 29; Acts 2: 16–18

6 All people that on earth do dwell

1 All people that on earth do dwell,
  Sing to the Lord with cheerful voice;
  Him serve with mirth, His praise forth tell;
  Come ye before Him and rejoice.

2 The Lord, ye know, is God indeed;
  Without our aid He did us make;
  We are His folk, He doth us feed;
  And for His sheep He doth us take.

3 O enter then His gates with praise;
  Approach with joy His courts unto;
  Praise, laud, and bless His name always,
  For it is seemly so to do.

4 For why? The Lord our God is good;
  His mercy is for ever sure;
  His truth at all times firmly stood,
  And shall from age to age endure.

William Kethe (d 1593)

7 *Amazing grace!*

early American melody

AMAZING GRACE

With feeling

Alto

A - maz - ing ___ grace! How sweet the sound That

Alto/
Descant

saved a ___ wretch like me; ___ I once ___ was ___ lost, but

now ___ am ___ found, Was blind, but ___ now I see. ___

Alto/Descant part: © Brenda Irene Piper

1 Amazing grace! How sweet the sound
That saved a wretch like me;
I once was lost, but now am found,
Was blind, but now I see.

2 'Twas grace that taught my heart to fear,
And grace my fears relieved;
How precious did that grace appear
The hour I first believed.

3 Through many dangers, toils and snares,
I have already come;
'Tis grace that brought me safe thus far,
And grace will lead me home.

4 When we've been there ten thousand years,
Bright shining as the sun,
We've no less days to sing God's praise
Than when we first begun.

John Newton (1725–1807)

8 Amen

spiritual

Capo 3(D)

With a swing

CHORUS

A - men, a - men,

A - men, a - men, a - men. *Fine*

VERSE

Verses 2, 3, 4 and 6

Verse 5

V.1. See the Ba - by Ly - ing in a

A - men, a - men,

man - ger One Christ-mas morn - ing.

A - men, a - men, a - men.

Start and finish with the chorus on its own.

10

Amen, amen,
Amen, amen, amen.

1   See the Baby
    Lying in a manger
    One Christmas morning.
        Amen, amen . . .

2   See Him in the temple
    Talking to the elders,
    Boy with head so wise,
        Amen, amen . . .

3   See Him by the lake-side
    Healing and a-preaching
    To the poor and sick.
        Amen, amen . . .

4   See Him in the garden
    Praying to the Father,
    Deep in His sorrow.
        Amen, amen . . .

5   Jesus was born,
    Born to die for all men;
    Now He lives again.
        Amen, amen . . .

6   Some day He's returning
    For all true believers,
    There'll be rejoicing.
        Amen, amen . . .

spiritual
Last verse: © *Brenda Irene Piper*

9 *And did those feet in ancient time*
(Jerusalem)

1 And did those feet in ancient time
Walk upon England's mountains green?
And was the holy Lamb of God
On England's pleasant pastures seen?
And did the countenance divine
Shine forth upon our clouded hills?
And was Jerusalem builded here
Among those dark satanic mills?

2 Bring me my bow of burning gold!
Bring me my arrows of desire!
Bring me my spear! O clouds, unfold!
Bring me my chariot of fire!
I will not cease from mental fight,
Nor shall my sword sleep in my hand,
Till we have built Jerusalem
In England's green and pleasant land.

William Blake (1757–1827)

10 A new commandment

A new commandment I give unto you
Is to love one another as I have loved you;
Is to love one another as I have loved you.
By this shall all men know you are my disciples:
If you have love one for another;
By this shall all men know you are my disciples:
If you have love one for another.

author unknown

John 13: 34, 35

11 Angels, from the realms of glory

1 Angels, from the realms of glory,
Wing your flight o'er all the earth;
Ye who sang creation's story
Now proclaim Messiah's birth:

Come and worship
Christ, the new-born King.
Come and worship,
Worship Christ, the new-born King.

2 Shepherds in the fields abiding,
Watching o'er your flocks by night,
God with man is now residing;
Yonder shines the infant Light:
Come and worship . . .

3 Sages, leave your contemplations;
Brighter visions beam afar;
Seek the great Desire of Nations;
Ye have seen His natal star:
Come and worship . . .

4 Saints before the altar bending,
Watching long in hope and fear,
Suddenly the Lord, descending,
In His temple shall appear:
Come and worship . . .

5 Though an infant now we view Him,
He shall fill His Father's throne,
Gather all the nations to Him,
Ev'ry knee shall then bow down:
Come and worship . . .

J. Montgomery (1771–1854)

12 At the name of Jesus

1 At the name of Jesus
  Ev'ry knee shall bow,
  Ev'ry tongue confess Him
  King of glory now.
  'Tis the Father's pleasure
  We should call Him Lord,
  Who from the beginning
  Was the mighty Word.

2 Humbled for a season,
  To receive a name
  From the lips of sinners
  Unto whom He came,
  Faithfully He bore it
  Spotless to the last,
  Brought it back victorious,
  When from death He passed:

3 Bore it up triumphant
  With its human light,
  Through all ranks of creatures,
  To the central height;
  To the throne of Godhead,
  To the Father's breast,
  Filled it with the glory
  Of that perfect rest.

4 In your hearts enthrone Him;
  There let Him subdue
  All that is not holy,
  All that is not true:
  Crown Him as your captain
  In temptation's hour,
  Let His will enfold you
  In its light and pow'r.

5 Brothers, this Lord Jesus
  Shall return again,
  With His Father's glory,
  With His angel-train;
  For all wreaths of empire
  Meet upon His brow,
  And our hearts confess Him
  King of glory now.

Caroline Noel (1817–77)

13 Away in a manger

1 Away in a manger, no crib for a bed,
The little Lord Jesus laid down His sweet head.
The stars in the bright sky looked down where He lay,
The little Lord Jesus asleep on the hay.

2 The cattle are lowing, the Baby awakes,
But little Lord Jesus no crying He makes.
I love Thee, Lord Jesus! Look down from the sky,
And stay by my side until morning is nigh.

3 Be near me, Lord Jesus; I ask Thee to stay
Close by me for ever, and love me, I pray.
Bless all the dear children in Thy tender care,
And fit us for heaven, to live with Thee there.

anonymous

14 Be Thou my vision

1 Be Thou my vision, O Lord of my heart,
   Be all else but naught to me, save that Thou art;
   Be Thou my best thought in the day and the night,
   Both waking and sleeping, Thy presence my light.

2 Be Thou my wisdom, be Thou my true word;
   Be Thou ever with me, and I with Thee, Lord;
   Be Thou my great Father, and I Thy true son;
   Be Thou in me dwelling, and I with Thee one.

3 Be Thou my breastplate, my sword for the fight;
   Be Thou my whole armour, be Thou my true might;
   Be Thou my soul's shelter, be Thou my strong tow'r:
   O raise Thou me heavenward, great pow'r of my pow'r.

4 Riches I need not, nor man's empty praise,
   Be Thou mine inheritance now and always;
   Be Thou and Thou only the first in my heart:
   O Sovereign of heaven, my treasure Thou art.

5 High King of heaven, Thou heaven's bright Sun,
   O grant me its joys after vict'ry is won;
   Great heart of my own heart, whatever befall,
   Still be Thou my vision, O Ruler of all.

ancient Irish, trans. Mary Elizabeth Byrne (1880–1931),
versified by Eleanor Henrietta Hull (1860–1935)

15 Bless the Lord, O my soul

composer unknown

KING OF KINGS
Majestically

Bless the Lord, O my soul, Bless the Lord, O my soul, And all that is with - in me bless His ho - ly name. Bless the name.

King of Kings,_____ Lord of Lords,_____ (for ev-er and ev-er) (for ev-er and ev-er)

King of Kings,_____ King of Kings and Lord of Lords. Bless the (for ev-er and ev-er) King of Kings and Lord of Lords. Bless the

18

Bless the Lord, O my soul,
Bless the Lord, O my soul,
And all that is within me bless His holy name.

Bless the Lord, O my soul,
Bless the Lord, O my soul,
And all that is within me bless His holy name.

King of Kings,
    (for ever and ever)
Lord of Lords,
    (for ever and ever)
King of Kings,
    (for ever and ever)
King of Kings and Lord of Lords.

Bless the Lord, O my soul,
Bless the Lord, O my soul,
And all that is within me bless His holy name.

author unknown

Psalm 103: 1

16 Book of books

1 Book of books, our people's strength,
   Statesman's, teacher's, hero's treasure,
   Bringing freedom, spreading truth,
   Shedding light that none can measure!
   Wisdom comes to those who know thee.
   All the best we have we owe thee.

2 Thank we those who toiled in thought,
   Many diverse scrolls completing,
   Poets, prophets, scholars, saints,
   Each his word from God repeating;
   Till they came, who told the story
   Of the Word, and showed His glory.

3 Praise we God, Who hath inspired
   Those whose wisdom still directs us,
   Praise Him for the Word made flesh,
   For the Spirit Who protects us.
   Light of knowledge, ever burning,
   Shed on us Thy deathless learning!

Percy Dearmer (1867–1936)

17 Bread and wine

1 Jesus said,
   'Eat this bread
   For my body giv'n,
   Eat this bread
   To show you've been forgiv'n;
   Eat this bread
   'Til again I come,
   Rememb'ring ev'rything I've done.'

2 Jesus said,
   'Drink this wine
   For the blood I've giv'n,
   Drink this wine
   To show you've been forgiv'n;
   Drink this wine
   'Til again I come,
   Rememb'ring ev'rything I've done.'

Brenda Irene Piper

Matt. 26: 26–30;
1 Cor. 11: 23–26

18 By Your Word

1 By Your Word, O Father, help me live,
   Write it in my heart and in my mind;
   May my life be, Lord, what You intend,
   For You're holy, just and kind.

2 By Your Word I want to live each day,
   Write it in my heart and in my mind;
   There is nothing else on which to build,
   There is nothing more to find.

3 By Your Word I'll live until I die,
   Keep it always in my heart and mind;
   May its truth direct me all my days,
   So my spirit be not blind.

Brenda Irene Piper

Hebrews 10: 15, 16

19 Come and praise the Lord our King

composer unknown

Triumphantly

Capo 2(C)

CHORUS: Come and praise the Lord our King, al - le - lu - ia, Come and praise the Lord our King, al - le - lu - ia.

VERSE: Christ was born in Beth - le - hem, al - le - lu - ia, Son of God and Son of Man: al - le - lu - ia.

Come and praise the Lord our King, alleluia,
Come and praise the Lord our King, alleluia.

1 Christ was born in Bethlehem, alleluia,
Son of God and Son of Man: alleluia.
Come and praise . . .

2 He grew up an earthly child, alleluia,
Of the world, but undefiled: alleluia.
Come and praise . . .

3 Jesus died at Calvary, alleluia,
Rose again triumphantly! alleluia.
Come and praise . . .

4 He will cleanse us from our sin, alleluia,
If we live by faith in Him: alleluia.
Come and praise . . .

5 We will live with Him one day, alleluia,
And for ever with Him stay: alleluia.
Come and praise . . .

author unknown

20 Christ is made the sure foundation

H. Purcell (1659–95)

WESTMINSTER ABBEY

Joyfully

Tune

Christ is made the sure found-a-tion, Christ the head and cor-ner - stone,

Descant

Chos-en of the Lord and pre-cious, Bind - ing all__the Church in one;

Ho - ly Zi - on's help for ev - er, And her con - fi - dence a - lone.

Descant: © Brenda Irene Piper

1 Christ is made the sure foundation,
   Christ the head and corner-stone,
   Chosen of the Lord and precious,
   Binding all the Church in one;
   Holy Zion's help for ever,
   And her confidence alone.

2 All that dedicated city
   Dearly loved of God on high,
   In exultant jubilation
   Pours perpetual melody,
   God the One in Three adoring
   In glad hymns eternally.

3 To this temple, where we call Thee,
   Come, O Lord of hosts, today;
   With Thy patient loving-kindness
   Hear Thy servants as they pray;
   And Thy fullest benediction
   Shed within its walls always.

4 Here please grant to all Thy servants
   What they ask of Thee to gain,
   What they gain from Thee for ever
   With the blessèd to retain,
   And hereafter in Thy glory
   Evermore with Thee to reign.

5 Praise and honour to the Father,
   Praise and honour to the Son,
   Praise and honour to the Spirit,
   Ever Three and ever One;
   One in might and One in glory,
   While unending ages run.

7th or 8th century,
trans. John Mason Neale (1818–66)

21 Come, ye thankful people, come

1 Come, ye thankful people, come,
Raise the song of harvest-home!
All be safely gathered in,
Ere the winter storms begin;
God, our Maker, doth provide
For our wants to be supplied;
Come to God's own temple, come;
Raise the song of harvest-home!

2 We ourselves are God's own field,
Fruit unto His praise to yield;
Wheat and tares together sown,
Unto joy or sorrow grown;
First the blade and then the ear,
Then the full corn shall appear;
Lord of harvest, grant that we
Wholesome grain and pure may be.

3 For the Lord our God shall come,
And shall take His harvest home;
From His field shall in that day
All offences purge away;
Give His angels charge at last
In the fire the tares to cast,
But the fruitful ears to store
In His garner evermore.

4 Then, thou Church triumphant, come,
  Raise the song of harvest-home;
  All be safely gathered in,
  Free from sorrow, free from sin,
  There, for ever purified
  In God's garner to abide;
  Come, ten thousand angels, come,
  Raise the glorious harvest-home!

H. Alford (1810–71)

22 Crown Him with many crowns

G.J. Elvey (1816–93)

DIADEMATA

Triumphantly

Crown Him with ma - ny crowns, The Lamb up - on His throne; Hark! how the heav'n-ly an - them drowns All mu - sic but its own: A - wake, my soul, and sing Of Him who died for thee, And hail Him as thy cho - sen King Through all e - ter - ni - ty.

Suggested accompaniment:
Brass and woodwind

1 Crown Him with many crowns,
The Lamb upon His throne;
Hark! how the heav'nly anthem drowns
All music but its own:
Awake, my soul, and sing
Of Him who died for thee,
And hail Him as thy chosen King
Through all eternity.

2 Crown Him the Son of God
Before the worlds began;
And ye who tread where He hath trod,
Crown Him the Son of Man,
Who ev'ry grief hath known
That wrings the human breast,
And takes and bears them for His own,
That all in Him may rest.

3 Crown Him the Lord of life,
Who triumphed o'er the grave,
And rose victorious in the strife,
For those He came to save:
His glories now we sing,
Who died and rose on high,
Who died eternal life to bring,
And lives that death may die.

4 Crown Him the Lord of heav'n,
Enthroned in worlds above;
Crown Him the King to whom is giv'n
The wondrous name of Love:
All hail, Redeemer, hail!
For Thou hast died for me;
Thy praise shall never, never fail
Throughout eternity.

Matthew Bridges (1800–94)
Godfrey Thring (1823–1903)

23 Dear Lord and Father of mankind

1 Dear Lord and Father of mankind,
   Forgive our foolish ways;
   Re-clothe us in our rightful mind;
   In purer lives Thy service find,
   In deeper rev'rence, praise,
   In deeper rev'rence, praise.

2 In simple trust like theirs who heard,
   Beside the Syrian sea,
   The gracious calling of the Lord,
   Let us, like them, without a word
   Rise up and follow Thee,
   Rise up and follow Thee.

3 O Sabbath rest by Galilee!
   O calm of hills above,
   Where Jesus knelt to share with Thee
   The silence of eternity,
   Interpreted by love,
   Interpreted by love!

4 With that deep hush subduing all
   Our words and works that drown
   The tender whisper of Thy call,
   As noiseless let Thy blessing fall
   As fell Thy manna down,
   As fell Thy manna down.

5 Drop Thy still dews of quietness,
   Till all our strivings cease;
   Take from our souls the strain and stress,
   And let our ordered lives confess
   The beauty of Thy peace,
   The beauty of Thy peace.

6 Breathe through the heats of our desire
   Thy coolness and Thy balm;
   Let sense be dumb, let flesh retire;
   Speak through the earthquake, wind and fire,
   O still small voice of calm,
   O still small voice of calm!

John Greenleaf Whittier (1807–92)

24 Eternal Father, strong to save

1 Eternal Father, strong to save,
Whose arm hath bound the restless wave,
Who bidd'st the mighty ocean deep
Its own appointed limits keep:
O hear us when we cry to Thee
For those in peril on the sea.

2 O Christ, whose voice the waters heard,
And hushed their raging at Thy word,
Who walkedst on the foaming deep,
And calm amid the storm didst sleep:
O hear us when we cry to Thee
For those in peril on the sea.

3 O Holy Spirit, who didst brood
Upon the chaos dark and rude,
And bid its angry tumult cease,
And give, for wild confusion, peace:
O hear us when we cry to Thee
For those in peril on the sea.

4 O Trinity of love and pow'r
Our brethren shield in danger's hour.
From rock and tempest, fire and foe,
Protect them whereso'er they go:
Thus evermore shall rise to Thee
Glad hymns of praise from land and sea.

William Whiting (1825–78), altered

25 Father, hear the prayer we offer

1 Father, hear the prayer we offer:
Not for ease that prayer shall be,
But for strength that we may ever
Live our lives courageously.

2 Not for ever in green pastures
Do we ask our way to be;
But the steep and rugged pathway
May we tread rejoicingly.

3 Not for ever by still waters
Would we idly rest and stay;
But would smite the living fountains
From the rocks along our way.

4 Be our strength in hours of weakness,
In our wand'rings be our guide;
Through endeavour, failure, danger,
Father, be Thou at our side.

Mrs L.M. Willis (1824–1908)

26 Fight the good fight

1 Fight the good fight with all thy might,
Christ is thy strength, and Christ thy right;
Lay hold on life, and it shall be
Thy joy and crown eternally.

2 Run the straight race through God's
good grace,
Lift up thine eyes and seek His face;
Life with its way before thee lies,
Christ is the path, and Christ the prize.

3 Cast care aside, lean on thy Guide,
His boundless mercy will provide;
Lean, and the trusting soul shall prove
Christ is its life, and Christ its love.

4 Faint not, nor fear, His arms are near,
He changeth not, and thou art dear;
Only believe, and thou shalt see
That Christ is all in all to thee.

John Samuel Bewley Monsell (1811–75)

27 Fill Thou my life

1 Fill Thou my life, O Lord my God,
  In ev'ry part with praise,
  That my whole being may proclaim
  Thy being and Thy ways.

2 Not for the lip of praise alone,
  Nor e'en the praising heart,
  I ask, but for a life made up
  Of praise in ev'ry part:

3 Praise in the common things of life,
  Its goings out and in;
  Praise in each duty and each deed,
  However small and mean.

4 Fill ev'ry part of me with praise;
  Let all my being speak
  Of Thee and of Thy love, O Lord,
  Poor though I be and weak.

5 So shalt Thou, Lord, from me, e'en me,
  Receive the glory due;
  And so shall I begin on earth
  The song for ever new.

6 So shall no part of day or night
  From sacredness be free;
  But all my life, in ev'ry step,
  Be fellowship with Thee.

Horatius Bonar (1808–89)

28 For all the blessings we have

Brenda Irene Piper

Introduction and interlude
Joyfully and with expression

Capo 5(C)

For all the bless-ings we have____ on this earth — O God we

thank You; For hope and Your prom-ise of life____ ev - er - more — We

give You thanks. For the glo - ri - ous sun____ that gives

poco a poco crescendo

warmth and light,__ For the air we breathe in both day and night, For the

Suggested accompaniment: Tom-toms, bongos or snaredrum

Words and music: © Brenda Irene Piper

34

joy of life mak-ing mu - sic bright – We thank You God.

For all the blessings we have on this earth –
O God we thank You;
For hope and Your promise of life evermore –
We give You thanks.

1 For the glorious sun that gives warmth and light,
For the air we breathe in both day and night,
For the joy of life making music bright –
We thank You God.
For all the blessings . . .

2 For the beauty around us seen very clear,
For enchanting sounds heard both far and near,
For the love of people to us so dear –
We thank You God.
For all the blessings . . .

3 For the food we enjoy to give strength each day,
For the clothes we wear ev'ry style and way,
For the homes we have for somewhere to stay –
We thank You God.
For all the blessings . . .

4 For the gift of Your Son who links us anew,
For forgiving us all the wrong we do,
For eternal life always close to You –
We thank You God.
For all the blessings . . .

Brenda Irene Piper

29 *For Your Holy Book we thank You*

1 For Your Holy Book we thank You,
And for all who served You well,
Writing, guarding and translating,
That its pages might forth tell
Your strong love and tender care
For Your people ev'rywhere.

2 For Your Holy Book we thank You
And for those who work today,
That the people of all nations,
Reading it and following, may
Know Your love and tender care
For Your people ev'rywhere.

3 For Your Holy Book we thank You,
May its message be our guide,
May we understand the wisdom
Of the laws it will provide,
And Your love and tender care
For Your people ev'rywhere.

Ruth Carter

30 *From all that dwell below the skies*

1 From all that dwell below the skies
Let the Creator's praise arise:
Alleluia! Alleluia!
Let the Redeemer's name be sung
Through ev'ry land, by ev'ry tongue:

Alleluia! Alleluia!
Alleluia! Alleluia! Alleluia!

2 Eternal are Thy mercies, Lord;
Eternal truth attends Thy word:
Alleluia! Alleluia!
Thy praise shall sound from shore to shore,
Till suns shall rise and set no more.
  Alleluia . . .

3 Your lofty themes, ye mortals, bring
In songs of praise divinely sing:
Alleluia! Alleluia!
The great salvation loud proclaim,
And shout for joy the Saviour's name.
  Alleluia . . .

4 In ev'ry land begin the song;
To ev'ry land the strains belong:
Alleluia! Alleluia!
In cheerful sounds all voices raise,
And fill the world with loudest praise.
  Alleluia . . .

Isaac Watts (1674–1748)

31 From the rising of the sun

From the rising of the sun
To the going down of the same,
The Lord's name is to be praised.
From the rising of the sun
To the going down of the same,
The Lord's name is to be praised.

Praise ye the Lord,
Praise Him O ye servants of the Lord,
Praise the name of the Lord,
Blessèd be the name of the Lord
From this time forth, and for evermore.

Paul Deming

Psalm 113: 3, 1, 2

32 Glorious things of thee are spoken

Glorious things of thee are spoken,
Zion, city of our God!
He, whose word cannot be broken,
Formed thee for His own abode:
On the Rock of Ages founded,
What can shake thy sure repose?
With salvation's walls surrounded,
Thou may'st smile at all thy foes.

2 See, the streams of living waters,
Springing from eternal love,
Well supply thy sons and daughters
And all fear of want remove:
Who can faint, while such a river
Ever flows their thirst to assuage?
Grace which, like the Lord, the Giver
Never fails from age to age.

3 Saviour, if of Zion's city
I, through grace, a member am,
Let the world deride or pity,
I will glory in Thy name:
Fading is the worldling's pleasure,
All his boasted pomp and show;
Solid joys and lasting treasure
None but Zion's children know.

John Newton (1725–1807)

33 God be in my head

God be in my head,
And in my understanding;
God be in mine eyes,
And in my looking;
God be in my mouth,
And in my speaking;
God be in my heart,
And in my thinking;
God be at mine end,
And at my departing.

Pynson's Horae (1514)

34 God in His love for us lent us this planet
(The stewardship of earth)

1 God in His love for us lent us this planet,
   Gave it a purpose in time and in space:
   Small as a spark from the fire of creation,
   Cradle of life and the home of our race.

2 Thanks be to God for its bounty and beauty,
   Life that sustains us in body and mind:
   Plenty for all, if we learn how to share it,
   Riches undreamed of to fathom and find.

3 Long have the wars of man ruined its harvest;
   Long has earth bowed to the terror of force;
   Long have we wasted what others have need of,
   Poisoned the fountain of life at its source.

4 Earth is the Lord's: it is ours to enjoy it,
   Ours, as His stewards, to farm and defend.
   From its pollution, misuse and destruction,
   Good Lord deliver us, world without end!

Fred Pratt Green

35 *God is working His purpose out*

1 God is working His purpose out
   As year succeeds to year;
   God is working His purpose out
   And the time is drawing near;
   Nearer and nearer draws the time,
   The time that shall surely be,
   When the earth shall be filled
   With the glory of God,
   As the waters cover the sea.

2 From utmost east to utmost west
   Where'er man's foot hath trod,
   By the mouth of many messengers
   Goes forth the voice of God:
   'Give ear to Me, ye continents,
   Ye isles, give ear to Me,
   That the earth may be filled
   With the glory of God,
   As the waters cover the sea.'

3 March we forth in the strength of God
   With the banner of Christ unfurled,
   That the light of the glorious gospel of truth
   May shine throughout the world;
   Fight we the fight with sorrow and sin,
   To set their captives free,
   That the earth may be filled
   With the glory of God,
   As the waters cover the sea.

4 All we can do is nothing worth
   Unless God blesses the deed;
   Vainly we hope for the harvest-tide
   Till God gives life to the seed;
   Yet nearer and nearer draws the time,
   The time that shall surely be,
   When the earth shall be filled
   With the glory of God,
   As the waters cover the sea.

Arthur Campbell Ainger (1841–1919)

36 God save our gracious Queen
(National Anthem)

1 God save our gracious Queen,
  Long live our noble Queen,
  God save the Queen!
  Send her victorious,
  Happy and glorious,
  Long to reign over us;
  God save the Queen!

2 Thy choicest gifts in store
  On her be pleased to pour,
  Long may she reign;
  May she defend our laws,
  And ever give us cause
  To sing with heart and voice,
  God save the Queen!

anonymous (c 1745)

37 Go tell it on the mountain

North American spiritual

Lively

Capo 5(C)

CHORUS

Go tell it on the moun - tain, ov - er the hills and ev - 'ry - where,___

Go tell it on the moun - tain that Je - sus Christ is born. While born.

Verses 1 and 2

VERSE (All verses)

Last time — *Fine*

shep-herds kept their watch-ing o'er wand-'ring flocks by night, Be -

- hold from out of hea - ven there shone a ho - ly light =___

D.C.

Suggested ostinato rhythm for percussion:

Go tell it on the mountain, over the hills and ev'rywhere,
Go tell it on the mountain that Jesus Christ is born.

1 While shepherds kept their watching o'er wand'ring flocks by night,
  Behold from out of heaven there shone a holy light –
    Go tell it . . .

2 And lo, when they had seen it, they all bowed down and prayed,
  They travelled on together to where the Babe was laid –
    Go tell it . . .

3 When I was a seeker, I sought both night and day;
  I asked my Lord to help me and He showed me the way –
    Go tell it . . .

4 He made me a watchman upon the city wall,
  And if I am a Christian, I am the least of all –
    Go tell it . . .

North American spiritual

38 Guide me, O Thou great Redeemer

J. Hughes (1873–1932)

CWM RHONDDA

With strength

Guide me, O Thou great Re - deem - er, Pil - grim through this
bar - ren land; I am weak, but Thou art migh - ty;
Hold me with Thy pow'r - ful hand: Bread of hea - ven,
Bread of hea - ven, Feed me now and ev - er - more, (ev - er-more)
Feed me now and ev - er - more.

Suggested accompaniment:
Brass and drums

1 Guide me, O Thou great Redeemer,
   Pilgrim through this barren land;
   I am weak, but Thou art mighty;
   Hold me with Thy pow'rful hand:
   Bread of heaven,
   Bread of heaven,
   Feed me now and evermore,
   Feed me now and evermore.

2 Open now the crystal fountain,
   Whence the healing stream doth flow;
   Let the fiery, cloudy pillar
   Lead me all my journey through:
   Strong Deliverer,
   Strong Deliverer,
   Be Thou still my strength and shield,
   Be Thou still my strength and shield.

3 When I tread the verge of Jordan,
   Bid my anxious fears subside;
   Death of death, and hell's destruction,
   Land me safe on Canaan's side:
   Songs of praises,
   Songs of praises
   I will ever give to Thee,
   I will ever give to Thee.

William Williams (1717–91), altered

39 Hallelujah! sing to Jesus

1 Hallelujah! sing to Jesus,
  His the sceptre, His the throne;
Hallelujah! His the triumph,
  His the victory alone;
Hark! the songs of peaceful Zion
  Thunder like a mighty flood;
Jesus out of ev'ry nation
  Hath redeemed us by His blood.

2 Hallelujah! not as orphans
  Are we left in sorrow now;
Hallelujah! He is near us,
  Faith believes, nor questions how;
Though the cloud from sight received Him
  When the forty days were o'er,
Shall our hearts forget His promise,
  'I am with you evermore'?

3 Hallelujah! Bread of angels,
  Thou on earth our food, our stay;
Hallelujah! here the sinful
  Flee to Thee from day to day;
Intercessor, Friend of sinners,
  Earth's Redeemer, plead for me,
Where the songs of all the sinless
  Sweep across the crystal sea.

4 Hallelujah! Hallelujah!
  Glory be to God on high;
To the Father, and the Saviour,
  Who has gained the victory;
Glory to the Holy Spirit,
  Fount of love and sanctity,
Hallelujah! Hallelujah!
  To the triune Majesty.

W.C. Dix (1837–98), altered

40 *Hark! the herald-angels sing*

1 Hark! the herald-angels sing
   Glory to the new-born King,
   Peace on earth, and mercy mild,
   God and sinners reconciled.
   Joyful, all ye nations, rise,
   Join the triumph of the skies;
   With the angelic host proclaim,
   'Christ is born in Bethlehem.'

   Hark! the herald-angels sing
   Glory to the new-born King.

2 Christ, by highest heav'n adored,
   Christ, the everlasting Lord,
   Late in time behold Him come,
   Offspring of a Virgin's womb.
   Veiled in flesh the Godhead see!
   Hail, the incarnate Deity!
   Pleased as Man with man to dwell,
   Jesus our Emmanuel.
     Hark! the herald-angels . . .

3 Hail, the heav'n-born Prince of Peace!
   Hail, the Sun of Righteousness!
   Light and life to all He brings,
   Ris'n with healing in His wings.
   Mild, He lays His glory by,
   Born that man no more may die,
   Born to raise the sons of earth,
   Born to give them second birth.
     Hark! the herald-angels . . .

     Charles Wesley (1707–88) and others

41 Heavenly Father, I appreciate You

1 Heavenly Father, I appreciate You,
Heavenly Father, I appreciate You.
I Love You, adore You,
I bow down before You,
Heavenly Father, I appreciate You.

2 Son of God, what a wonder You are,
Son of God, what a wonder You are.
Our souls You cleanse from sin,
Your Spirit then comes in,
Son of God, what a wonder You are.

3 Holy Ghost, what a comfort You are,
Holy Ghost, what a comfort You are.
You lead us, You guide us,
You live right inside us,
Holy Ghost, what a comfort You are.

author unknown

42 He is Lord

composer unknown

Tune

Triumphantly
D   D7   G (C)   G

He is Lord.   He is Lord.   He is
(He is Lord)   (He is Lord)

Alto

G   A   D   D7 G G7

ris-en from the dead and He is Lord.   Ev-'ry knee shall bow, ev-'ry
(He is Lord)

C   Am   G/D   D7   G (C) G

tongue con - fess That Je - sus Christ is Lord.
(He is Lord)

He is Lord. He is Lord.
He is risen from the dead and He is Lord.
Ev'ry knee shall bow, ev'ry tongue confess
That Jesus Christ is Lord.

author unknown

Philippians 2: 9, 10, 11

Alto part: © Brenda Irene Piper

43 He's got the whole wide world in His hands

With a swing

He's got the whole wide world_____ in His hands, He's got the
big round world_____ in His hands, He's got the whole wide world____
____ in His hands, He's got the whole world in His hands._____

Suggested ostinato rhythm for percussion:

1 He's got the whole wide world in His hands,
   He's got the big round world in His hands,
   He's got the whole wide world in His hands,
   He's got the whole world in His hands.

2 He's got the wind and the rain in His hands,
   He's got the sun and the moon in His hands,
   He's got the wind and the rain in His hands,
   He's got the whole world in His hands.

52

3 He's got that tiny little baby in His hands,
   He's got that helpless little baby in His hands,
   He's got that tiny little baby in His hands,
   He's got the whole world in His hands.

4 He's got you and me, brother, in His hands,
   He's got you and me, sister, in His hands,
   He's got you and me, brother, in His hands,
   He's got the whole world in His hands.

5 He's got ev'rybody in His hands,
   He's got ev'rybody in His hands,
   He's got ev'rybody in His hands,
   He's got the whole world in His hands.

spiritual

44 *His hands were pierced*

1 His hands were pierced, the hands that made
   The mountain range and everglade;
   That washed the stains of sin away
   And changed earth's darkness into day.

2 His feet were pierced, the feet that trod
   The furthest shining star of God;
   And left their imprint deep and clear
   On ev'ry winding pathway here.

3 His heart was pierced, the heart that burned
   To comfort ev'ry heart that yearned;
   And from it came a cleansing flood,
   The river of redeeming blood.

4 His hands and feet and heart, all three
   Were pierced for me on Calvary;
   And here and now, to Him I bring
   My hands, feet, heart, an offering.

D. Wood
from The Victorious Christ

45 *His name is higher*

composer unknown

Chime bars part: © Brenda Irene Piper

than an-y oth - er,____ His name is Je - sus,____ His name is Lord.____

His name is higher than any other,
His name is Jesus, His name is Lord;
His name is higher than any other,
His name is Jesus, His name is Lord.
His name is Wonderful, His name is Counsellor,
His name is Prince of Peace, the Mighty God;
His name is higher than any other,
His name is Jesus, His name is Lord.

author unknown

Isaiah 9: 6

46 *His name is wonderful*

His name is wonderful,
His name is wonderful,
His name is wonderful,
Jesus my Lord;
He is the mighty King,
Master of ev'rything,
His name is wonderful,
Jesus my Lord.

He's the great Shepherd,
The Rock of all ages,
Almighty God is He;
Bow down before Him,
Love and adore Him,
His name is wonderful,
Jesus my Lord!

author unknown

47 *Holy, holy, holy is the Lord*

composer unknown

Capo 2(G)

Ho-ly, ho-ly, ho-ly is the Lord; Ho-ly is the Lord God Al-

(ho-ly) (ho-ly)

1st time | 2nd time

- migh - ty! ty! Who was, and is, and is to

come: Ho - ly, ho - ly, ho - ly is the Lord!___

(ho - ly) (ho - ly)

56

1 Holy, holy, holy is the Lord;
   Holy is the Lord God Almighty!
   Holy, holy, holy is the Lord;
   Holy is the Lord God Almighty!
   Who was, and is, and is to come:
   Holy, holy, holy is the Lord!

2 Jesus, Jesus, Jesus is the Lord;
   Jesus is the Lord God Almighty!
   Jesus, Jesus, Jesus is the Lord;
   Jesus is the Lord God Almighty!
   Who was, and is, and is to come:
   Holy, holy, holy is the Lord!

3 Worthy, worthy, worthy is the Lord;
   Worthy is the Lord God Almighty!
   Worthy, worthy, worthy is the Lord;
   Worthy is the Lord God Almighty!
   Who was, and is, and is to come:
   Holy, holy, holy is the Lord!

4 Glory, glory, glory to the Lord;
   Glory to the Lord God Almighty!
   Glory, glory, glory to the Lord;
   Glory to the Lord God Almighty!
   Who was, and is, and is to come:
   Holy, holy, holy is the Lord!

author unknown

Revelation 4: 8

48 How good is the God we adore!

1 How good is the God we adore!
   Our faithful, unchangeable friend;
   His love is as great as His pow'r
   And knows neither measure nor end.

2 For Christ is the First and the Last,
   His Spirit will guide us safe home;
   We'll praise Him for all that is past
   And trust Him for all that's to come.

Joseph Hart (1712–68)

49 How great is our God

composer unknown

Capo 3(D)

Tune

Joyfully

F (D)   C7 (A7)

How great is our God, _____ how great is His

Alto

(How great is our God,)

F (D)   Bb (G)   F (D)   C7 (A7)

name, _____ How great is His love _____ for ev-er the

(how great is His name,)   (How great is His love)

F (D)   Bb (G)   F (D)   F7 (D7)

same. _____ He rolled back the wa - ters _____

(for ev - er the same.)   (He rolled back the

of the migh-ty Red Sea, _____ And He said, 'I'll nev-er

wa - ters) (of the migh-ty Red Sea,)

leave you, _____ put your trust in Me.' _____

(And He said, 'I'll nev-er leave you,) (put your trust in Me.')

How great is our God, how great is His name,
How great is His love for ever the same.
He rolled back the waters of the mighty Red Sea,
And He said, 'I'll never leave you, put your trust in Me.'

author unknown

50 *How lovely on the mountains*
(Our God reigns)

1 How lovely on the mountains are the feet of Him
Who brings good news, good news,
Proclaiming peace, announcing news of happiness,
Our God reigns, our God reigns.

Our God reigns, our God reigns,
Our God reigns, our God reigns.

2 You watchmen lift your voices joyfully as one,
Shout for your King, your King.
See eye to eye the Lord restoring Zion:
Your God reigns, your God reigns!
  Our God reigns . . .

3 Waste places of Jerusalem break forth with joy,
We are redeemed, redeemed.
The Lord has saved and comforted His people:
Your God reigns, your God reigns!
  Our God reigns . . .

4 Ends of the earth, see the salvation of your God,
Jesus is Lord, is Lord.
Before the nations He has bared His holy arm:
Your God reigns, your God reigns!
  Our God reigns . . .

L. E. Smith Jnr.

51 How sweet the name of Jesus sounds

1 How sweet the name of Jesus sounds
In a believer's ear!
It soothes his sorrows, heals his wounds,
And drives away his fear.

2 It makes the wounded spirit whole,
And calms the troubled breast;
'Tis manna to the hungry soul,
And to the weary, rest.

3 Dear name! the rock on which I build,
My shield and hiding-place,
My never-failing treasury, filled
With boundless stores of grace.

4 Jesus! my Shepherd, Saviour, Friend,
My Prophet, Priest, and King;
My Lord, my Life, my Way, my End,
Accept the praise I bring.

5 Weak is the effort of my heart,
And cold my warmest thought;
But when I see Thee as Thou art,
I'll praise Thee as I ought.

6 Till then I would Thy love proclaim
With ev'ry fleeting breath;
And may the music of Thy name
Refresh my soul in death!

John Newton (1725–1807)

52 If I had a hammer

1 If I had a hammer, I'd hammer in the morning,
   I'd hammer in the evening, all over this land;
   I'd hammer out danger, I'd hammer out a warning,
   I'd hammer out love between my brothers and my sisters,
   All over this land.

2 If I had a bell, I'd ring it in the morning,
   I'd ring it in the evening, all over this land;
   I'd ring out danger, I'd ring out a warning,
   I'd ring out love between my brothers and my sisters,
   All over this land.

3 If I had a song, I'd sing it in the morning,
   I'd sing it in the evening, all over this land;
   I'd sing out danger, I'd sing out a warning,
   I'd sing out love between my brothers and my sisters,
   All over this land.

4 Well I've got a hammer, and I've got a bell,
   And I've got a song to sing all over this land;
   It's the hammer of justice, it's the bell of freedom,
   It's the song about love between my brothers and my sisters,
   All over this land.

Pete Seeger and Lee Hays

53 I'm so glad

Brenda Irene Piper

Introduction
Joyfully

I'm so glad,
God loves ev-'ry-bo-dy, I'm so glad, He loves ev-'ry-one; I'm so glad,
I'm so glad God's love is for - ev - er! - er!

Suggested ostinato rhythm for a snare drum:

1 I'm so glad, God loves ev'rybody,
   I'm so glad, He loves ev'ryone;
   I'm so glad, I'm so glad
   God's love is forever!

2 I'm so glad, God's love gave us Jesus,
   I'm so glad, God saw hope in Him;
   I'm so glad, I'm so glad
   There is hope forever!

3 I'm so glad, Jesus died to save us,
   I'm so glad, His blood cleanses sin;
   I'm so glad, I'm so glad
   He can cleanse forever!

4 I'm so glad, Jesus is arisen,
   I'm so glad, He's alive today;
   I'm so glad, I'm so glad
   He's alive forever!

5 I'm so glad, heaven's door is open,
   I'm so glad, life there can be mine;
   I'm so glad, I'm so glad
   I can live forever!

Brenda Irene Piper

54 In heavenly love abiding

1 In heav'nly love abiding,
No change my heart shall fear;
And safe is such confiding,
For nothing changes here:
The storm may roar without me,
My heart may low be laid;
But God is round about me,
And can I be dismay'd?

2 Wherever He may guide me,
No want shall turn me back;
My Shepherd is beside me,
And nothing can I lack:
His wisdom ever waketh,
His sight is never dim;
He knows the way He taketh,
And I will walk with Him.

3 Green pastures are before me,
Which yet I have not seen;
Bright skies will soon be o'er me,
Where darkest clouds have been:
My hope I cannot measure,
My path to life is free;
My Saviour has my treasure,
And He will walk with me.

Anna Laetitia Waring (1820–1910)

55 In the bleak mid-winter

1 In the bleak mid-winter
Frosty wind made moan;
Earth stood hard as iron,
Water like a stone;
Snow had fallen, snow on snow,
Snow on snow,
In the bleak mid-winter,
Long ago.

2 Our God, heav'n cannot hold Him
Nor earth sustain;
Heav'n and earth shall flee away
When He comes to reign;
In the bleak mid-winter
A stable-place sufficed
The Lord God Almighty,
Jesus Christ.

3 Enough for Him, whom cherubim
Worship night and day,
A breastful of milk,
And a mangerful of hay;
Enough for Him, whom angels
Fall down before,
The ox and ass and camel
Which adore.

4 Angels and archangels
May have gathered there,
Cherubim and seraphim
Thronged the air;
But only His mother
In her maiden bliss
Worshipped the Belovèd
With a kiss.

5 What can I give Him,
Poor as I am?
If I were a shepherd
I would bring a lamb;
If I were a wise man
I would do my part;
Yet what I can I give Him –
Give my heart.

Christina Rossetti (1830–94)

56 In the name of Jesus

In the name of Jesus,
In the name of Jesus,
We have the victory;
In the name of Jesus,
In the name of Jesus,
Demons will have to flee.

Who can tell what God can do?
Who can tell of His love for you?
In the name of Jesus, Jesus,
We have the victory!

author unknown

Luke 10: 17

57 I vow to thee, my country

1 I vow to thee, my country, all earthly things above,
   Entire and whole and perfect, the service of my love:
   The love that asks no question, the love that stands the test,
   That lays upon the altar the dearest and the best;
   The love that never falters, the love that pays the price,
   The love that makes undaunted the final sacrifice.

2 And there's another country, I've heard of long ago,
   Most dear to them that love her, most great to them that know;
   We may not count her armies, we may not see her King;
   Her fortress is a faithful heart, her pride is suffering;
   And soul by soul and silently her shining bounds increase,
   And her ways are ways of gentleness and all her paths are peace.

Sir Cecil Spring Rice (1859–1918)

58 I want to worship the Lord

I want to worship the Lord with all of my heart,
Give Him my all and not just a part;
Lift up my hands to the King of Kings,
Praise Him in ev'rything.

author unknown

59 I will enter His gates

I will enter His gates with thanksgiving in my heart,
I will enter His courts with praise,
I will say this is the day that the Lord has made,
I will rejoice for He has made me glad.

He has made me glad, He has made me glad,
I will rejoice for He has made me glad.
He has made me glad, He has made me glad,
I will rejoice for He has made me glad.

author unknown

Psalm 100: 4; 118: 24

60 *I will sing the wondrous story*

R.H. Prichard (1811–87)

HYFRYDOL

Capo 5(C)

Joyfully

I will sing____ the won - drous sto - ry
How He left____ the realms of glo - ry

Of the Christ who died____ for me, Yes, I'll
For the cross on Cal - va - ry.

sing____ the won - drous sto - ry Of the Christ__ who

died____ for me, Sing__ it with__ His saints__ in

glo - ry, Gath - ered by____ the cry - stal sea.

1 I will sing the wondrous story
  Of the Christ who died for me,
  How He left the realms of glory
  For the cross on Calvary.
  Yes, I'll sing the wondrous story
  Of the Christ who died for me,
  Sing it with His saints in glory,
  Gathered by the crystal sea.

2 I was lost: but Jesus found me,
  Found the sheep that went astray,
  Raised me up and gently led me
  Back into the narrow way.
  Days of darkness still may meet me,
  Sorrow's paths I oft may tread;
  But His presence still is with me,
  By His guiding hand I'm led.

3 He will keep me till the river
  Rolls its waters at my feet,
  Then He'll bear me safely over,
  All my joys in Him complete.
  Yes, I'll sing the wondrous story
  Of the Christ who died for me,
  Sing it with His saints in glory,
  Gathered by the crystal sea.

F.H. Rawley (1854–1952)

61 I will sing unto the Lord

I will sing unto the Lord as long as I live,
I will sing praise to my God while I have my being.
My meditation of Him shall be sweet,
I will be glad, I will be glad in the Lord.

Bless thou the Lord, O my soul,
Praise ye the Lord.
Bless thou the Lord, O my soul,
Praise ye the Lord.
Bless thou the Lord, O my soul,
Praise ye the Lord.
Bless thou the Lord, O my soul,
Praise ye the Lord.

Donya Brockway

Psalm 104: 33, 34, 35b

62 Jesus calls us; o'er the tumult

1 Jesus calls us; o'er the tumult
   Of our life's wild restless sea,
   Day by day His voice is sounding,
   Saying, 'Christian, follow me.'

2 As, of old, apostles heard it
   By the Galilean lake,
   Turned from home, and toil, and kindred,
   Leaving all for His dear sake.

3 Jesus calls us from the worship
   Of the vain world's golden store,
   From each idol that would keep us,
   Saying, 'Christian, love Me more.'

4 In our joys and in our sorrows,
   Days of toil and hours of ease,
   Still He calls, in cares and pleasures,
   'Christian, love Me more than these.'

5 Jesus calls us! By Thy mercies,
   Saviour, may we hear Thy call,
   Give our hearts to Thine obedience,
   Serve and love Thee best of all.

Mrs C.F. Alexander (1818–95)

63 Jesus Christ is risen today

1 Jesus Christ is ris'n today, Alleluia!
Our triumphant holy day, Alleluia!
Who did once, upon the cross, Alleluia!
Suffer to redeem our loss. Alleluia!

2 Hymns of praise then let us sing, Alleluia!
Unto Christ, our heav'nly King, Alleluia!
Who endured the cross and grave, Alleluia!
Sinners to redeem and save. Alleluia!

3 But the pains that He endured, Alleluia!
Our salvation have procured; Alleluia!
Now above the sky He's King, Alleluia!
Where the angels ever sing. Alleluia!

Lyra Davidica (1708) and the Supplement (1816)

Matt. 28: 7; Heb. 12: 2

64 Jesus, Name above all names

Jesus, Name above all names.
Beautiful Saviour, Glorious Lord,
Emmanuel, God is with us,
Blessèd Redeemer, Living Word.

Naida Hearn

Philippians 2: 9

65 Jesus shall reign

1 Jesus shall reign where'er the sun
 Does his successive journeys run;
 His kingdom stretch from shore to shore
 Till moons shall rise and set no more.

2 To Him shall endless prayer be made,
 And princes throng to crown His head;
 His name like sweet perfume shall rise
 With ev'ry morning sacrifice.

3 People and realms of ev'ry tongue
 Dwell on His love with sweetest song;
 And infant voices shall proclaim
 Their early blessings on His name.

4 Blessings abound where'er He reigns;
 The prisoner leaps to lose his chains,
 The weary find eternal rest,
 And all the sons of want are blessed.

5 Let ev'ry creature rise and bring
 The highest honours to our King;
 Angels descend with songs again,
 And earth repeat the loud Amen.

Isaac Watts (1674–1748) altered

66 Jesus, Thou joy of loving hearts

1 Jesus, Thou joy of loving hearts,
   Thou Fount of Life, Thou Light of men,
   From the best bliss that earth imparts
   We turn unfilled to Thee again.

2 Thy truth unchanged hath ever stood;
   Thou savest those that on Thee call;
   To them that seek Thee Thou art good,
   To them that find Thee, all in all.

3 We taste Thee, O Thou Living Bread,
   And long to feast upon Thee still;
   We drink of Thee, the Fountain-head,
   And thirst our souls from Thee to fill.

4 Our restless spirits yearn for Thee,
   Where'er our changeful lot is cast;
   Glad when Thy gracious smile we see,
   Blessed when our faith can hold Thee fast.

5 O Jesus, ever with us stay;
   Make all our moments calm and bright;
   Chase the dark night of sin away;
   Shed o'er the world Thy holy light.

12th-century Latin, trans. Ray Palmer (1808–87)

67 *Joy to the world!*

arr. from G.F. Handel (1685–1759)

Joy to the world! The Lord is come; Let earth re-
-ceive her King; Let ev - 'ry__ heart__ pre - pare__ Him__
room,__ And heav'n and na - ture__ sing, And__ heav'n and na - ture__
sing, And__ heav'n, and heav'n__ and na - ture sing.

Suggested ostinato rhythm for percussion:

1 Joy to the world! The Lord is come;
   Let earth receive her King;
   Let ev'ry heart prepare Him room,
   And heav'n and nature sing,
   And heav'n and nature sing,
   And heav'n, and heav'n and nature sing.

2 Joy to the world! The Saviour reigns;
   Let men their songs employ;
   While fields and floods, rocks, hills and plains
   Repeat the sounding joy,
   Repeat the sounding joy,
   Repeat, repeat the sounding joy.

3 He rules the world with truth and grace,
   And makes the nations prove
   The glories of His righteousness,
   And wonders of His love,
   And wonders of His love,
   And wonders, and wonders of His love,

Isaac Watts (1674–1748)

68 *Just a closer walk with Thee*

traditional

Tune / **Alto**

With feeling

CHORUS: Just a clo - ser walk with Thee,
VERSE: I am weak but Thou art strong,

(walk with Thee)
(Thou art strong)

Grant it, Je - sus, if You please;_____ Dai - ly walk-ing close with
Je - sus keep me from all wrong;_____ I'll be sat - is - fied as

(if You please)
(from all wrong)

Thee,_____ Let it be, dear Lord, let it be.
long_____ As I walk, dear Lord, close to Thee.

(close to Thee)
(just as long)

(let it be)
(close to Thee)

Just a closer walk with Thee,
Grant it, Jesus, if You please;
Daily walking close with Thee,
Let it be, dear Lord, let it be.

1 I am weak but Thou art strong,
Jesus keep me from all wrong;
I'll be satisfied as long
As I walk, dear Lord, close to Thee.
    Just a closer walk . . .

2 Through this world of toil and snares,
If I falter, Lord, who cares?
Who with me my burden shares?
None but Thee, dear Lord, none but Thee.
    Just a closer walk . . .

3 When my feeble life is o'er,
Time for me will be no more,
Guide me gently, safely home
To Thy Kingdom's shore, to Thy shore.
    Just a closer walk . . .

traditional

69 Kum ba yah
(Come by here)

Kum is pronounced 'Koom'.

1 Kum ba yah, my Lord, Kum ba yah,
Kum ba yah, my Lord, Kum ba yah,
Kum ba yah, my Lord, Kum ba yah,
O Lord, Kum ba yah.

2 Someone's crying, Lord, Kum ba yah,
Someone's crying, Lord, Kum ba yah,
Someone's crying, Lord, Kum ba yah,
O Lord, Kum ba yah.

3 Someone's singing, Lord, Kum ba yah,
Someone's singing, Lord, Kum ba yah,
Someone's singing, Lord, Kum ba yah,
O Lord, Kum ba yah.

4 Someone's praying, Lord, Kum ba yah,
Someone's praying, Lord, Kum ba yah,
Someone's praying, Lord, Kum ba yah,
O Lord, Kum ba yah.

5 Hear our prayer, O Lord, hear our prayer,
Keep our friends, O Lord, in your care,
Keep our friends, O Lord, in your care,
O Lord, hear our prayer.

traditional

(Other intercessory verses may be added . . . .
Someone's hungry . . . . lonely . . . .
wounded . . . . dying, etc.)

70 Lead us, heavenly Father

1 Lead us, heav'nly Father, lead us
O'er the world's tempestuous sea;
Guard us, guide us, keep us, feed us,
For we have no help but Thee;
Yet possessing ev'ry blessing
If our God our Father be.

2 Saviour, breathe forgiveness o'er us,
All our weakness Thou dost know;
Thou didst tread this earth before us,
Thou didst feel its keenest woe;
Lone and dreary, faint and weary,
Through the desert Thou didst go.

3 Spirit of our God, descending,
Fill our hearts with heav'nly joy,
Love with ev'ry passion blending,
Pleasure that can never cloy:
Thus provided, pardoned, guided,
Nothing can our peace destroy.

J. Edmeston (1791–1867)

71 *Let all the world*

1 Let all the world in ev'ry corner sing
'My God and King!'
The heav'ns are not too high;
His praise may thither fly:
The earth is not too low;
His praises there may grow.
Let all the world in ev'ry corner sing
'My God and King!'

2 Let all the world in ev'ry corner sing
'My God and King!'
The Church with psalms must shout,
No door can keep them out:
But, above all, the heart
Must bear the longest part.
Let all the world in ev'ry corner sing
'My God and King!'

George Herbert (1593–1633)

72 Lord, behold us with Thy blessing

1 Lord, behold us with Thy blessing,
Once again assembled here;
Onward be our footsteps pressing,
In Thy love and faith and fear:
Still protect us,
Still protect us
By Thy presence ever near.

2 For Thy mercy we adore Thee,
For this rest upon our way,
Lord, again we bow before Thee,
Speed our labours day by day:
Mind and spirit,
Mind and spirit
With Thy choicest gifts array.

3 Keep the spell of home affection
Still alive in ev'ry heart;
May its pow'r, with mild direction,
Draw our love from self apart,
Till Thy children,
Till Thy children
Feel that Thou their Father art.

H.J. Buckoll (1803–71)

73 Lord, dismiss us with Thy blessing

1 Lord, dismiss us with Thy blessing;
Thanks for mercies past receive;
Pardon all, their faults confessing;
Time that's lost may all retrieve:
May Thy children,
May Thy children
Ne'er again Thy Spirit grieve.

2 Bless Thou all our days of leisure,
Help us selfish lures to flee;
Sanctify our ev'ry pleasure;
Pure and blameless may it be:
May our gladness,
May our gladness
Draw us evermore to Thee.

3 Let Thy father-hand be shielding
All who here shall meet no more;
May their seed-time past be yielding
Year by year a richer store:
Those returning,
Those returning
Make more faithful than before.

H.J. Buckoll (1803–71)

74 Lord Jesus Christ, You have come to us
(Living Lord)

1 Lord Jesus Christ, You have come to us,
You are one with us, Mary's Son;
Cleansing our souls from all their sin,
Pouring Your love and goodness in,
Jesus, our love for You we sing,
Living Lord.

2 Lord Jesus Christ, now and ev'ry day,
Teach us how to pray, Son of God.
You have commanded us to do
This in remembrance, Lord, of You;
Into our lives Your pow'r breaks through,
Living Lord.

3 Lord Jesus Christ, You have come to us,
Born as one of us, Mary's Son;
Led out to die on Calvary,
Risen from death to set us free;
Living Lord Jesus, help us see
You are Lord.

4 Lord Jesus Christ, we would come to You,
Live our lives for You, Son of God;
All Your commands we know are true;
Your many gifts will make us new;
Into our lives Your pow'r breaks through,
Living Lord.

Patrick Appleford (b 1925)

75 Lord of heaven and earth

(A young person's prayer)

1 Lord of heaven and earth,
 You breathed in me at my birth;
 Life is never straight-forward here,
 Will You make it to me clear?

2 Lord, whenever I pray
 Whether during night or day,
 It is hard to know where to start
 To tell all within my heart.

3 Lord, You know ev'rything,
 And You hear these words I sing;
 Help me know the truth about You,
 And the things You'd have me do.

4 Lord, now into Your hand
 Take my life while here I stand,
 After years pass by may I see
 How Your hand has guided me.

Brenda Irene Piper

76 Lord, speak to me

1 Lord, speak to me, that I may speak
  In living echoes of Thy tone;
  As Thou has sought, so let me seek
  Thy erring children lost and lone.

2 O lead me, Lord, that I may lead
  The wand'ring and the wav'ring feet;
  O feed me, Lord, that I may feed
  Thy hung'ring ones with manna sweet.

3 O strengthen me, that, while I stand
  Firm on the rock, and strong in Thee,
  I may stretch out a loving hand
  To wrestlers with the troubled sea.

4 O teach me, Lord, that I may teach
  The precious things Thou dost impart;
  And wing my words, that they may reach
  The hidden depths of many a heart.

5 O give Thine own sweet rest to me,
  That I may speak with soothing pow'r
  A word in season, as from Thee,
  To weary ones in needful hour.

6 O fill me with Thy fulness, Lord,
  Until my very heart o'erflow
  In kindling thought and glowing word,
  Thy love to tell, Thy praise to show.

7 O use me, Lord, use even me,
  Just as Thou wilt, and when, and where,
  Until Thy blessèd face I see,
  Thy rest, Thy joy, Thy glory share.

Frances Ridley Havergal (1836–79)

77 Lord, Thy kingdom bring triumphant

1 Lord, Thy kingdom bring triumphant,
   Give this world Thy liberty,
   May Thy Spirit's strong compulsion
   Rule our tides of energy:

2 Where the vessel cleaves the ocean,
   Or the pilot steers his plane,
   Where the miner toils in darkness,
   And the farmer sows the grain.

3 Consecrate Thy people's labour
   At the airfield, mill and port;
   With the gladness of Thy presence
   Bless our homes and grace our sport.

4 Let Thy mercy and Thy wisdom
   Rule our courts and parliament,
   And to soldier, sage and scholar
   May Thy light and truth be sent.

5 By the pioneer's endeavour,
   By the word of printed page,
   By the martyr's dying witness,
   And Thy saints in ev'ry age:

6 By the living voice of preacher,
   By the skill of surgeon's hand,
   By the far born broadcast tidings
   Speaking peace from land to land:

7 Lord, Thy kingdom bring triumphant,
   Visit us this living hour,
   Let Thy toiling, sinning children
   See Thy kingdom come in pow'r.

A.F. Bayly (b 1901)

78 Lord, You have searched and known me

1 Lord, You have searched and known me,
There's nothing within me You cannot see,
You know ev'rything about my ways
Throughout my days.

Open my heart and into me pour
Your love and wisdom, Lord, more and more,
Open my mind that I may know
Your plan for me while here below.

2 Even before words are on my tongue,
And even before any deed is done,
You know, mighty Lord, all that lies before
And evermore.
        Open my heart . . .

3 Lord, You have formed all my inward part,
You knit me together right from the start,
You know me far more than I know myself:
Come be my help.
        Open my heart . . .

4 Knowing myself means first knowing You,
And seeking Your will, Lord, in all I do,
Just take my whole being and fashion me
Like You to be.
        Open my heart . . .

5 Lord, make me more like Yourself I pray,
Please help me Your will always to obey,
My thoughts of You, Lord, are all filled with praise
For all Your ways.
        Open my heart . . .

Brenda Irene Piper

Psalm 139

79 Love divine

1 Love divine, all loves excelling,
Joy of heav'n, to earth come down,
Fix in us Thy humble dwelling,
All Thy faithful mercies crown:
Jesus, Thou art all compassion,
Pure, unbounded love Thou art;
Visit us with Thy salvation,
Enter ev'ry trembling heart.

2 Breathe, O breathe Thy loving Spirit
Into ev'ry troubled breast;
Let us all in Thee inherit,
Let us find Thy promised rest;
Take away the love of sinning,
Alpha and Omega be;
End of faith, as its beginning,
Set our hearts at liberty.

3 Come, Almighty to deliver,
Let us all Thy grace receive;
Suddenly return, and never,
Never more Thy temples leave.
Thee we would be always blessing,
Serve Thee as Thy hosts above,
Pray, and praise Thee without ceasing,
Glory in Thy perfect love.

4 Finish, then, Thy new creation:
Pure and spotless let us be;
Let us see Thy great salvation,
Perfectly restored in Thee,
Changed from glory into glory,
Till in heaven we take our place,
Till we cast our crowns before Thee,
Lost in wonder, love, and praise.

Charles Wesley (1707—88)

80 Majesty

Majesty, worship His Majesty;
Unto Jesus be glory, honour and praise.
Majesty, kingdom, authority
Flow from His throne unto His own,
His anthem raise.

So exalt, lift up on high the name of Jesus,
Magnify, come glorify Christ Jesus the King.
Majesty, worship His Majesty,
Jesus who died, now glorified,
King of all kings.

Jack W. Hayford

Revelation 1: 5, 6

81 Man of Sorrows!

1 Man of Sorrows! What a name
For the Son of God, who came
Ruined sinners to reclaim!
Hallelujah! What a Saviour!

2 Bearing shame and scoffing rude,
In my place condemned He stood;
Sealed my pardon with His blood:
Hallelujah! What a Saviour!

3 Guilty, vile, and helpless, we;
Spotless Lamb of God was He:
Full atonement – can it be?
Hallelujah! What a Saviour!

4 Lifted up was He to die,
'It is finished!' was His cry;
Now in heav'n exalted high:
Hallelujah! What a Saviour!

5 When He comes, our glorious King,
All His ransomed home to bring,
Then anew this song we'll sing:
Hallelujah! What a Saviour!

Philipp Bliss (1838–76)

Isaiah 53: 3-9;
John 19: 30;
1 Thess. 4: 16, 17

82 Morning has broken

old Gaelic melody

BUNESSAN

Flowing

C · Dm · G · F · C

Tune

Morn-ing has bro - ken   Like the   first morn - ing,

Alto

C · Em · Am · D7 · Gsus4 · G7 · C · F

Black-bird has spo - ken   Like the first bird.____   Praise for the sing - ing!

C · Am · G · C · Em · F · G · Csus4 · C

Praise for the morn - ing!   Praise for them, spring - ing   Fresh from the Word!__

Suggested accompaniment:
flute (tune) and clarinet (alto) for last verse

From *The Children's Bells*, published by Oxford Univeristy Press.
Alto part: © Brenda Irene Piper

1 Morning has broken
  Like the first morning,
  Blackbird has spoken
  Like the first bird.
  Praise for the singing!
  Praise for the morning!
  Praise for them, springing
  Fresh from the Word!

2 Sweet the rain's new fall
  Sunlit from heaven,
  Like the first dewfall
  On the first grass.
  Praise for the sweetness
  Of the wet garden,
  Sprung in completeness
  Where His feet pass.

3 Mine is the sunlight!
  Mine is the morning
  Born of the one light
  Eden saw play!
  Praise with elation,
  Praise ev'ry morning,
  God's re-creation
  Of the new day!

  Eleanor Farjeon (1881–1965)

83 Mine eyes have seen the glory

melody attributed to
William Steffe

BATTLE HYMN

Capo 2(G)

Victory march

VERSE

Mine eyes have seen the glo - ry of the com - ing of the Lord; He is
tramp - ling out the vin - tage where the grapes of wrath are stored; He hath
loosed the fate - ful light - ning of His ter - ri - ble swift sword. His
truth is march - ing on. Glo - ry, glo - ry, Hal - le -
lu - jah! Glo - ry, glo - ry, Hal - le - lu - jah!
Glo - ry, glo - ry, Hal - le - lu - jah! His truth is march - ing on.

Suggested ostinato rhythm for percussion:

94

1 Mine eyes have seen the glory of the coming of the Lord;
  He is trampling out the vintage where the grapes of wrath are stored;
  He hath loosed the fateful lightning of His terrible swift sword:
  His truth is marching on.

  Glory, glory, Hallelujah!
  Glory, glory, Hallelujah!
  Glory, glory, Hallelujah!
  His truth is marching on.

2 I've seen Him in the watch-fires of a hundred circling camps,
  They have builded Him an altar in the evening dews and damps;
  I have read His righteous sentence by the dim and flaring lamps:
  His day is marching on.
      Glory, glory . . .

3 He hath sounded forth the trumpet that shall never call retreat;
  He is sifting out the hearts of men before His judgement seat:
  O, be swift, my soul, to answer Him: be jubilant, my feet!
  Our God is marching on.
      Glory, glory . . .

4 In the beauty of the lilies Christ was born, across the sea,
  With a glory in His bosom that transfigures you and me;
  As He died to make men holy, let us live to make men free,
  While God is marching on.
      Glory, glory . . .

Julia Ward Howe (1819–1910)

84 *My song is love unknown*

1 My song is love unknown,
My Saviour's love to me:
Love to the loveless shown,
That they might lovely be.
O who am I,
That for my sake
My Lord should take
Frail flesh, and die?

2 He came from His blest throne
Salvation to bestow;
But men made strange, and none
The longed-for Christ would know:
But O, my Friend,
My Friend indeed,
Who at my need
His life did spend.

3 Sometimes they strew His way,
And His sweet praises sing;
Resounding all the day
Hosannas to their King:
Then 'Crucify!'
Is all their breath,
And for His death
They thirst and cry.

4 They rise and needs will have
  My dear Lord made away;
  A murderer they save,
  The Prince of Life they slay;
  Yet steadfast He
  To suff'ring goes,
  That He His foes
  From thence might free.

5 In life, no house, no home
  My Lord on earth might have;
  In death, no friendly tomb,
  But what a stranger gave.
  What may I say?
  Heav'n was His home,
  But mine the tomb
  Wherein He lay.

6 Here might I stay and sing,
  No story so divine;
  Never was love, dear King!
  Never was grief like Thine.
  This is my Friend,
  In whose sweet praise
  I all my days
  Could gladly spend.

Samuel Crossman (1624–83)

85 New life

Brenda Irene Piper

Introduction, interlude and coda
With life and expression

Capo 5(C)

VERSE New life, new life our Fa - ther gives To the seeds, the pips and stones; New

life, new life our Fa - ther gives, And each one of them He owns. CHORUS New

Tune life, new life Our Fa-ther gives a - bun - dant - ly; New

Descant (new life) (new life)

1 New life, new life our Father gives
To the seeds, the pips and stones;
New life, new life our Father gives,
And each one of them He owns.

New life, new life
Our Father gives abundantly;
New life, new life,
And it's there for you and me.

2 New life, new life our Father gives
To the bulbs that sprout up tall;
New life, new life our Father gives,
Adding colour to them all.
New life . . .

3 New life, new life our Father gives
To the plants, the shrubs and trees;
New life, new life our Father gives,
And each bud He knows and sees.
New life . . .

4 New life, new life our Father gives
To the eggs both large and small;
New life, new life our Father gives,
And He knows about them all.
New life . . .

5 New life, new life our Father gives
When each caterpillar dies;
New life, new life our Father gives,
So they live as butterflies.
New life . . .

6 New life, new life our Father gives
To each person who loves Him;
New life, new life our Father gives,
When our hearts He enters in.
New life . . .

Brenda Irene Piper

86 Now thank we all our God

1 Now thank we all our God,
   With hearts and hands and voices,
   Who wondrous things hath done,
   In whom His world rejoices;
   Who, from our mother's arms
   Hath blessed us on our way
   With countless gifts of love,
   And still is ours today.

2 O may this bounteous God
   Through all our life be near us,
   With ever-joyful hearts
   And blessèd peace to cheer us;
   And keep us in His grace,
   And guide us when perplexed,
   And free us from all ills
   In this world and the next.

3 All praise and thanks to God
   The Father now be given,
   The Son, and Him who reigns
   With them in highest heaven,
   The one eternal God,
   Whom earth and heav'n adore;
   For thus it was, is now,
   And shall be evermore.

Martin Rinckart (1586–1649),
trans. Catherine Winkworth (1827–78)

87 O come, all ye faithful

1 O come, all ye faithful,
   Joyful and triumphant,
   O come ye, O come ye to Bethlehem,
   Come and behold Him,
   Born the King of angels:

   O come, let us adore Him,
   O come, let us adore Him,
   O come, let us adore Him,
   Christ the Lord!

2 Child, for us sinners,
   Poor and in the manger,
   Fain we embrace Thee, with love and awe;
   Who would not love Thee,
   Loving us so dearly?
   O come . . .

3 Sing, choirs of angels,
   Sing in exultation,
   Sing, all ye citizens of heaven above;
   Glory to God
   In the highest:
   O come . . .

4 Yea, Lord, we greet Thee,
   Born this happy morning,
   Jesu, to Thee be glory giv'n;
   Word of the Father,
   Now in flesh appearing:
   O come . . .

trans. Frederick Oakeley (1802–80)

88 *O for a thousand tongues to sing*

T. Jarman (1782–1862)

LYNGHAM

Capo 5(C)

Triumphantly

O for a thou - sand tongues to sing My great Re - deem - er's praise, My great Re - deem - er's praise! The glo - ries of my God and King, The tri - umphs of His grace, The

The tri - umphs of His grace, The tri - umphs of His

tri-umphs of His grace, The tri - umphs of His grace!

grace, The tri-umphs of His grace, The tri-umphs of His grace!

1 O for a thousand tongues to sing
  My great Redeemer's praise,
  My great Redeemer's praise!
  The glories of my God and King,
  The triumphs of His grace,
  The triumphs of His grace,
  The triumphs of His grace!

2 Jesus! the name that charms our fears,
  That bids our sorrows cease,
  That bids our sorrows cease;
  'Tis music in the sinner's ears,
  'Tis life, and health, and peace,
  'Tis life, and health, and peace,
  'Tis life, and health, and peace.

3 See all your sins on Jesus laid;
  The Lamb of God was slain,
  The Lamb of God was slain;
  His soul was once an off'ring made
  For ev'ry soul of man,
  For ev'ry soul of man,
  For ev'ry soul of man.

4 He breaks the pow'r of cancelled sin,
  He sets the pris'ner free,
  He sets the pris'ner free;
  His blood can make the foulest clean,
  His blood availed for me,
  His blood availed for me,
  His blood availed for me.

5 He speaks, and, list'ning to His voice,
  New life the dead receive,
  New life the dead receive,
  The mournful, broken hearts rejoice,
  The humble poor believe,
  The humble poor believe,
  The humble poor believe.

6 Hear Him, ye deaf; His praise, ye dumb,
  Your loosened tongues employ,
  Your loosened tongues employ;
  Ye blind, behold your Saviour come;
  And leap, ye lame, for joy,
  And leap, ye lame, for joy,
  And leap, ye lame, for joy!

7 My gracious Master and my God,
  Assist me to proclaim,
  Assist me to proclaim,
  To spread through all the earth abroad
  The honours of Thy name,
  The honours of Thy name,
  The honours of Thy name.

Charles Wesley (1707–88)

89 O God, our help in ages past

1 O God, our help in ages past,
  Our hope for years to come,
  Our shelter from the stormy blast,
  And our eternal home.

2 Beneath the shadow of Thy throne
  Thy saints have dwelt secure;
  Sufficient is Thine arm alone,
  And our defence is sure.

3 Before the hills in order stood,
  Or earth received her frame,
  From everlasting Thou art God,
  To endless years the same.

4 A thousand ages in Thy sight
  Are like an ev'ning gone,
  Short as the watch that ends the night
  Before the rising sun.

5 Time, like an ever-rolling stream,
  Bears all its sons away;
  They fly forgotten, as a dream
  Dies at the op'ning day.

6 O God, our help in ages past,
  Our hope for years to come,
  Be Thou our guard while troubles last
  And our eternal home.

Isaac Watts (1674–1748)

90 O Jesus, I have promised

1 O Jesus, I have promised
  To serve Thee to the end;
  Be Thou for ever near me,
  My Master and my Friend:
  I shall not fear the battle
  If Thou art by my side,
  Nor wander from the pathway
  If Thou wilt be my Guide.

2 O let me feel Thee near me:
  The world is ever near;
  I see the sights that dazzle,
  The tempting sounds I hear;
  My foes are ever near me,
  Around me and within;
  But, Jesus, draw Thou nearer,
  And shield my soul from sin.

3 O let me hear Thee speaking
  In accents clear and still,
  Above the storms of passion,
  The murmurs of self-will;
  O speak to reassure me,
  To hasten or control;
  O speak, and make me listen,
  Thou Guardian of my soul.

4 O Jesus, Thou hast promised,
  To all who follow Thee,
  That where Thou art in glory
  There shall Thy servant be;
  And, Jesus, I have promised
  To serve Thee to the end;
  O give me grace to follow
  My Master and my Friend.

5 O let me see Thy footmarks,
  And in them plant mine own;
  My hope to follow duly
  Is in Thy strength alone:
  O guide me, call me, draw me,
  Uphold me to the end;
  And then in heav'n receive me,
  My Saviour and my Friend!

J.E. Bode (1816–74)

91 O Lord my God!

(How great Thou art)

1 O Lord my God! When I in awesome wonder
Consider all the works Thy hand hath made,
I see the stars, I hear the mighty thunder,
Thy pow'r throughout the universe displayed:

Then sings my soul, my Saviour God, to Thee,
How great Thou art! How great Thou art!
Then sings my soul, my Saviour God, to Thee,
How great Thou art! How great Thou art!

2 When through the woods and forest glades I wander
And hear the birds sing sweetly in the trees;
When I look down from lofty mountain grandeur,
And hear the brook, and feel the gentle breeze:
  Then sings my soul . . .

3 And when I think that God His Son not sparing,
Sent Him to die – I scarce can take it in.
That on the cross my burden gladly bearing,
He bled and died to take away my sin:
  Then sings my soul . . .

4 When Christ shall come with shout of acclamation
And take me home – what joy shall fill my heart!
Then shall I bow in humble adoration
And there proclaim, my God, how great Thou art!
  Then sings my soul . . .

translated from the Russian by Stuart K. Hine

92 Once in royal David's city

1 Once in royal David's city
Stood a lowly cattle shed,
Where a mother laid her Baby
In a manger for His bed.
Mary was that mother mild,
Jesus Christ her little Child.

2 He came down to earth from heaven,
Who is God and Lord of all,
And His shelter was a stable,
And His cradle was a stall.
With the poor, and mean, and lowly,
Lived on earth our Saviour holy.

3 And through all His wondrous childhood
He would honour and obey,
Love and watch the lowly maiden
In whose gentle arms He lay.
Christian children all must be
Mild, obedient, good as He.

4 For He is our childhood's pattern,
Day by day like us He grew,
He was little, weak, and helpless,
Tears and smiles like us He knew;
And He feeleth for our sadness,
And He shareth in our gladness.

5 And our eyes at last shall see Him,
Through His own redeeming love,
For that Child so dear and gentle
Is our Lord in heav'n above;
And He leads His children on
To the place where He is gone.

Mrs C.F. Alexander (1818–95)

93 Only Jesus

1 Who took fish and bread, hungry people fed?
   Who changed water into wine?
   Who made well the sick, who made see the blind?
   Who touched earth with feet divine?
   Only Jesus, only Jesus, only He has done this:
   Who made live the dead? Truth and kindness spread?
   Only Jesus did all this.

2 Who walked dusty road? Cared for young and old?
   Who sat children on His knee?
   Who spoke words so wise? Filled men with surprise,
   Who gave all, but charged no fee?
   Only Jesus, only Jesus, only He has done this:
   Who in death and grief spoke peace to a thief?
   Only Jesus did all this.

3 Who soared through the air? Joined His Father there?
   He has you and me in view:
   He, who this has done, is God's only Son,
   And He's int'rested in you.
   Only Jesus, only Jesus, only He has done this:
   He can change a heart, give a new fresh start,
   Only He can do all this.

Betty Lou Mills

94 Onward, Christian soldiers!

1 Onward, Christian soldiers!
Marching as to war,
With the cross of Jesus
Going on before.
Christ the royal Master
Leads against the foe;
Forward into battle,
See, His banners go!

Onward, Christian soldiers!
Marching as to war,
With the cross of Jesus
Going on before.

2 Crowns and thrones may perish,
Kingdoms rise and wane,
But the Church of Jesus
Constant will remain;
Gates of hell can never
'Gainst that Church prevail;
We have Christ's own promise,
And that cannot fail:
Onward . . .

3 Onward, then, ye people,
Join our happy throng,
Blend with ours your voices
In the triumph song;
Glory, praise, and honour
Unto Christ the King;
This through countless ages
Men and angels sing:
Onward . . .

S. Baring-Gould (1834–1924)

95 Peace is flowing like a river

1 Peace is flowing like a river,
Flowing out through you and me,
Spreading out into the desert,
Setting all the captives free.

Let it flow through me,
Let it flow through me,
Let the mighty peace of God flow out through me;
Let it flow through me,
Let it flow through me,
Let the mighty peace of God flow out through me.

2 Love is flowing . . .
Let it flow . . .

3 Joy is flowing . . .
Let it flow . . .

4 Faith is flowing . . .
Let it flow . . .

5 Hope is flowing . . .
Let it flow . . .

author unknown

96 Praise God, from whom all blessings flow

(Doxology)

Thomas Tallis (1505–85)

TALLIS' CANON

Majestically

This can be sung as a four-part round unaccompanied or with
the following chordal accompaniment repeated throughout:

Praise God, from whom all blessings flow;
Praise Him, all creatures here below,
Praise Him above, ye heav'nly host;
Praise Father, Son and Holy Ghost.

Thomas Ken (1637–1711)

97 Praise Him!

1 Praise Him! Praise Him!
   Praise Him in the morning,
   Praise Him in the noon-time,
   Praise Him! Praise Him!
   Praise Him when the sun goes down.

2 Jesus! Jesus!
   Jesus in the morning,
   Jesus in the noon-time,
   Jesus! Jesus!
   Jesus when the sun goes down.

3 Love Him! Love Him!
   Love Him in the morning,
   Love Him in the noon-time,
   Love Him! Love Him!
   Love Him when the sun goes down.

4 Trust Him! Trust Him!
   Trust Him in the morning,
   Trust Him in the noon-time,
   Trust Him! Trust Him!
   Trust Him when the sun goes down.

5 Serve Him! Serve Him!
   Serve Him in the morning,
   Serve Him in the noon-time,
   Serve Him! Serve Him!
   Serve Him when the sun goes down.

author unknown

98 Praise, my soul, the King of heaven

1 Praise, my soul, the King of heaven;
  To His feet thy tribute bring;
  Ransomed, healed, restored, forgiven,
  Who like thee His praise should sing?
  Praise Him! Praise Him! Praise Him! Praise Him!
  Praise the everlasting King.

2 Praise Him for His grace and favour
  To our fathers in distress;
  Praise Him, still the same for ever,
  Slow to chide, and swift to bless:
  Praise Him! Praise Him! Praise Him! Praise Him!
  Glorious in His faithfulness.

3 Father-like He tends and spares us;
  Well our feeble frame He knows;
  In His hands He gently bears us,
  Rescues us from all our foes:
  Praise Him! Praise Him! Praise Him! Praise Him!
  Widely as His mercy flows.

4 Angels, help us to adore Him!
  Ye behold Him face to face;
  Sun and moon, bow down before Him;
  Dwellers all in time and space:
  Praise Him! Praise Him! Praise Him! Praise Him!
  Praise with us the God of grace.

H.F. Lyte (1793–1847)

99 Praise the Lord in the beauty of holiness

Praise the Lord in the beauty of holiness
For He is our God,
And His mercy endureth for ever
For He is our God.

(Sing through twice)

author unknown

2 Chronicles 20: 21

100 Praise to the Lord, the Almighty

1 Praise to the Lord, the Almighty, the King of creation;
   O my soul, praise Him, for He is thy health and salvation:
   All ye who hear,
   Brothers and sisters, draw near,
   Praise Him in glad adoration.

2 Praise to the Lord, who o'er all things so wondrously reigneth,
   Shelters thee under His wings, yea, so gently sustaineth:
   Hast thou not seen?
   All that is needful hath been
   Granted in what He ordaineth.

3 Praise to the Lord, who doth prosper thy work, and defend thee!
   Surely His goodness and mercy here daily attend thee:
   Ponder anew
   What the Almighty can do,
   Who with His love doth befriend thee.

4 Praise to the Lord! O let all that is in me adore Him!
   All that hath life and breath come now with praises before Him!
   Let the amen
   Sound from His people again:
   Gladly for aye we adore Him.

Joachim Neander (1650–80),
trans. Catherine Winkworth (1827–78) and others

101 Put your hand in the hand

1 Put your hand in the hand of the Man
   who stilled the water.
   Put your hand in the hand of the Man
   who calmed the sea.
   Take a look at yourself and you can look
   at others diff'rently,
   By puttin' your hand in the hand of the Man
   from Galilee.

2 Ev'ry time I look into the Holy Book
   I want to tremble.
   When I read about the part where a carpenter
   cleared the temple.
   For the buyers and the sellers were no diff'rent
   fellas than what I profess to be,
   And it causes me pain to know we're not the people
   we should be.

3 Put your hand in the hand of the Man
   who stilled the water.
   Put your hand in the hand of the Man
   who calmed the sea.
   Take a look at yourself and you can look
   at others diff'rently,
   By puttin' your hand in the hand of the Man
   from Galilee.

Gene MacLellan

102 Rejoice, the Lord is King!

G.F. Handel (1685–1759)

GOPSAL

Majestically

Re - joice, the Lord is King! Your Lord and__King a - dore; Mor -

- tals, give thanks and sing, And tri - umph ev - er - more: *Lift*

up your heart, lift up your voice; Re-joice! A - gain, I__say: re - joice!

Suggested accompaniment:
Brass

1 Rejoice, the Lord is King!
Your Lord and King adore;
Mortals, give thanks and sing,
And triumph evermore:

Lift up your heart, lift up your voice;
Rejoice! Again, I say: rejoice!

2 Jesus the Saviour reigns,
The God of truth and love;
When He had purged our stains,
He took His seat above:
Lift up your heart . . .

3 His kingdom cannot fail,
He rules o'er earth and heav'n;
The keys of death and hell
Are to our Jesus giv'n:
Lift up your heart . . .

4 He sits at God's right hand
Till all His foes submit,
And bow to His command,
And fall beneath His feet:
Lift up your heart . . .

5 Rejoice in glorious hope;
Jesus the Judge shall come,
And take His servants up
To their eternal home:

We soon shall hear the archangel's voice;
The trump of God shall sound: rejoice!

Charles Wesley (1707–88)

103 Rejoice in the Lord always

composer unknown

This is a round in four parts.

Capo 1(E)

Rejoice in the Lord always,
And again I say, rejoice!
Rejoice in the Lord always,
And again I say, rejoice!

Rejoice, rejoice, and again I say, rejoice!
Rejoice, rejoice, and again I say, rejoice!

author unknown

Philippians 4: 4

104 Rock of ages, cleft for me

1 Rock of ages, cleft for me,
Let me hide myself in Thee;
Let the water and the blood,
From Thy riven side which flowed,
Be of sin the double cure,
Cleanse me from its guilt and pow'r.

2 Not the labour of my hands
Can fulfil Thy law's demands;
Could my zeal no respite know,
Could my tears for ever flow,
All for sin could not atone:
Thou must save, and Thou alone.

3 Nothing in my hand I bring,
Simply to Thy cross I cling;
Naked, come to Thee for dress;
Helpless, look to Thee for grace;
Foul, I to the fountain fly:
Wash me, Saviour, or I die.

4 While I draw this fleeting breath,
When mine eyes shall close in death,
When I soar through tracts unknown,
See Thee on Thy judgement throne,
Rock of ages, cleft for me,
Let me hide myself in Thee.

A.M. Toplady (1740–78)

105 See, amid the winter's snow

J. Goss (1800–80)

OXFORD

With feeling

See, a-mid the win-ter's snow, Born for us on earth be-low;

See, the ten-der Lamb ap-pears, Prom-ised from e - ter - nal years:

CHORUS

Hail, thou ev - er - bless - èd morn; Hail, re-demp-tion's hap - py dawn;

Sing through all Je - ru - sa-lem, Christ is born in Beth - le - hem.

Suggested instruments for descant: recorders, flutes or violins

Descant: © Brenda Irene Piper

1 See, amid the winter's snow,
  Born for us on earth below;
  See, the tender Lamb appears,
  Promised from eternal years:

  Hail, thou ever-blessèd morn;
  Hail, redemption's happy dawn;
  Sing through all Jerusalem,
  Christ is born in Bethlehem.

2 Lo, within a manger lies
  He who built the starry skies;
  He who throned in height sublime
  Sits amid the cherubim.
    Hail, thou ever-blessèd . . .

3 Say, ye holy shepherds, say
  What your joyful news today;
  Wherefore have ye left your sheep
  On the lonely mountain steep?
    Hail, thou ever-blessèd . . .

4 'As we watched at dead of night,
  Lo, we saw a wondrous light;
  Angels singing 'Peace on earth'
  Told us of the Saviour's birth:'
    Hail, thou ever-blessèd . . .

5 Sacred Infant, all divine,
  What a tender love was Thine,
  Thus to come from highest bliss
  Down to such a world as this:
    Hail, thou ever-blessèd . . .

6 Teach, O teach us, Holy Child,
  By Thy face so meek and mild,
  Teach us to resemble Thee
  In Thy sweet humility:
    Hail, thou ever-blessèd . . .

E. Caswall (1814–78)

121

106 Silent night

1 Silent night, holy night!
   All is calm, all is bright,
   Round yon virgin mother and Child.
   Holy Infant, so tender and mild,
   Sleep in heavenly peace,
   Sleep in heavenly peace.

2 Silent night, holy night!
   Shepherds quake at the sight,
   Glories stream from heaven afar,
   Heav'nly hosts sing 'Alleluia',
   Christ the Saviour is born,
   Christ the Saviour is born.

3 Silent night, holy night!
   Son of God, love's pure light
   Radiant beams from Thy holy face
   With the dawn of redeeming grace,
   Jesus, Lord, at Thy birth,
   Jesus, Lord, at Thy birth.

Joseph Mohr (1792–1848),
trans. Stopford Brooke (1832–1916)

107 Standing in the need of prayer

Negro spiritual

Capo 5(C)

With a swing

Tune / Descant

CHORUS

It's me, it's me, O Lord, stand-ing in the need of prayer; It's
(it's me)

me, it's me, O Lord, stand-ing in the need of prayer. Not my
(it's me)

bro-ther nor my sis-ter but it's me, O Lord, stand-ing in the need of prayer; Not my

bro-ther nor my sis-ter but it's me, O Lord, stand-ing in the need of prayer.

VERSE

It's me, it's me, O Lord, standing in the need of prayer;
It's me, it's me, O Lord, standing in the need of prayer.

1 Not my brother nor my sister but it's me, O Lord,
      standing in the need of prayer;
   Not my brother nor my sister but it's me, O Lord,
      standing in the need of prayer.
      It's me, it's me, O Lord . . .

2 Not my mother nor my father but it's me, O Lord,
      standing in the need of prayer;
   Not my mother nor my father but it's me, O Lord,
      standing in the need of prayer.
      It's me, it's me, O Lord . . .

3 Not the preacher nor my leader but it's me, O Lord,
      standing in the need of prayer;
   Not the preacher nor my leader but it's me, O Lord,
      standing in the need of prayer.
      It's me, it's me, O Lord . . .

4 Not the stranger nor my neighbour but it's me, O Lord,
      standing in the need of prayer;
   Not the stranger nor my neighbour but it's me, O Lord,
      standing in the need of prayer.
      It's me, it's me, O Lord . . .

Negro spiritual

108 Surely goodness and mercy

1 A pilgrim was I, and a-wand'ring,
In the cold night of sin I did roam,
When Jesus the kind Shepherd found me,
And now I am on my way home.

Surely goodness and mercy shall follow me
All the days, all the days of my life;
Surely goodness and mercy shall follow me
All the days, all the days of my life.
And I shall dwell in the house of the Lord for ever,
And I shall feast at the table spread for me;
Surely goodness and mercy shall follow me
All the days, all the days of my life,
All the days, all the days of my life. (after last verse only)

2 He restoreth my soul when I'm weary,
He giveth me strength day by day;
He leads me beside the still waters,
He guards me each step of the way.
Surely goodness and mercy . . .

3 When I walk through the dark lonesome valley,
My Saviour will walk with me there;
And safely His great hand will lead me
To the mansions He's gone to prepare.
Surely goodness and mercy . . .

John W. Peterson

Psalm 23

109 Take my life

1 Take my life, and let it be
Consecrated, Lord, to Thee;
Take my moments and my days,
Let them flow in ceaseless praise.

2 Take my hands, and let them move
At the impulse of Thy love;
Take my feet, and let them be
Swift and beautiful for Thee.

3 Take my voice, and let me sing
Always, only, for my King;
Take my lips, and let them be
Filled with messages from Thee.

4 Take my silver and my gold,
Not a mite would I withhold;
Take my intellect, and use
Ev'ry power as Thou shalt choose.

5 Take my will, and make it Thine;
It shall be no longer mine;
Take my heart, it is Thine own;
It shall be Thy royal throne.

6 Take my love; my Lord, I pour
At Thy feet its treasure store;
Take myself, and I will be
Ever, only, all, for Thee.

Frances Ridley Havergal (1836–79)

110 Tell out, my soul

1 Tell out, my soul, the greatness of the Lord!
Unnumbered blessings give my spirit voice;
Tender to me the promise of His word –
In God my Saviour shall my heart rejoice.

2 Tell out, my soul, the greatness of His name!
Make known His might, the deeds His arm has done;
His mercy sure, from age to age the same –
His Holy Name: the Lord, the Mighty One.

3 Tell out, my soul, the greatness of His might!
Pow'rs and dominions lay their glory by.
Proud hearts and stubborn wills are put to flight,
The hungry fed, the humble lifted high.

4 Tell out, my soul, the glories of His word!
Firm is His promise, and His mercy sure.
Tell out, my soul, the greatness of the Lord
To children's children and for evermore!

Timothy Dudley-Smith

111 Thank You

1 Thank You for ev'ry new good morning,
  Thank You for ev'ry fresh new day,
  Thank You that I may cast my burdens
  Wholly on to You.

2 Thank You for ev'ry friend I have, Lord,
  Thank You for ev'ry one I know,
  Thank You when I can feel forgiveness
  To my greatest foe.

3 Thank You for leisure and for schooling,
  Thank You for ev'ry heartfelt joy,
  Thank You for all that makes me happy
  And for melody.

4 Thank You for ev'ry shade and sorrow,
  Thank You for comfort in Your Word,
  Thank You that I am guided by You
  Ev'rywhere I go.

5 Thank You for grace to know Your gospel,
  Thank You for all Your Spirit's pow'r,
  Thank You for Your unfailing love
  Which reaches far and near.

6 Thank You for free and full salvation,
  Thank You for grace to hold it fast,
  Thank You, O Lord, I want to thank You
  That I'm free to thank!
  Thank You, O Lord, I want to thank You
  That I'm free to thank!

M.G. Schneider, trans. and
adapted by S. Lonsdale and M.A. Baughen

112 The day Thou gavest, Lord, is ended

1 The day Thou gavest, Lord, is ended,
The darkness falls at Thy behest;
To Thee our morning hymns ascended,
Thy praise shall sanctify our rest.

2 We thank Thee that Thy Church unsleeping,
While earth rolls onward into light,
Through all the world her watch is keeping,
And rests not now by day or night.

3 As o'er each continent and island
The dawn leads on another day,
The voice of prayer is never silent,
Nor dies the strain of praise away.

4 The sun that bids us rest is waking
Our brethren 'neath the western sky,
And hour by hour fresh lips are making
Thy wondrous doings heard on high.

5 So be it, Lord; Thy throne shall never,
Like earth's proud empires, pass away;
Thy kingdom stands, and grows for ever,
Till all Thy creatures own Thy sway.

John Ellerton (1826–93)

113 The Bible tells of God's great plan

1 The Bible tells of God's great plan
For people ev'rywhere,
That all should learn to live in love
And in His kingdom share.

2 He sent His Son, Lord Jesus Christ
To show His love for all,
And many people followed Christ
In answer to His call.

3 As God spoke then to men of old,
So still He speaks today,
We pray that we may learn His will
And follow in His way.

W.L. Jenkins

114 The head that once was crowned with thorns

1 The head that once was crowned
    with thorns
Is crowned with glory now:
A royal diadem adorns
The mighty Victor's brow.

2 The highest place that heav'n affords
Is His by sov'reign right:
The King of kings and Lord of lords,
He reigns in perfect light.

3 The joy of all who dwell above,
The joy of all below,
To whom He manifests His love,
And grants His name to know.

4 To them the cross, with all its shame,
With all its grace, is giv'n:
Their name an everlasting name,
Their joy the joy of heav'n.

5 They suffer with their Lord below;
They reign with Him above;
Their profit and their joy, to know
The myst'ry of His love.

6 The cross He bore is life and health,
Though shame and death to Him;
His people's hope, His people's wealth,
Their everlasting theme.

Thomas Kelly (1769–1854)

115 The Lord's my Shepherd

Jessie S. Irvine (1836–87)

CRIMOND

Capo 3(D)

The Lord's my Shepherd, I'll not want; He makes me down to lie In pastures green; He leadeth me The quiet waters by.

1 The Lord's my Shepherd, I'll not want;
  He makes me down to lie
  In pastures green; He leadeth me
  The quiet waters by.

2 My soul He doth restore again,
  And me to walk doth make
  Within the paths of righteousness,
  E'en for His own name's sake.

3 Yea, though I walk through death's dark vale,
  Yet will I fear no ill;
  For Thou art with me, and Thy rod
  And staff me comfort still.

4 My table Thou hast furnishèd
  In presence of my foes;
  My head Thou dost with oil anoint,
  And my cup overflows.

5 Goodness and mercy all my life
  Shall surely follow me;
  And in God's house for evermore
  My dwelling-place shall be.

Francis Rous (1579–1659),
revised for Scottish Psalter (1650)

Psalm 23

116 The Lord's prayer

Our Father, who art in heav'n,
Hallowèd be Thy name.
Thy kingdom come,
Thy will be done,
On earth, as it is in heav'n.
Give us this day our daily bread,
And forgive us our trespasses,
As we forgive them that trespass against us.
And lead us not into temptation,
But deliver us from evil.
For Thine is the kingdom, the power and the glory,
For ever and ever,
Amen.

Matthew 6: 9–13

117 The Lord's prayer (Caribbean)

1 Our Father, who art in heaven,
  Hallowèd be Thy name!
  Thy Kingdom come, Thy will be done,
  Hallowèd be Thy name!

2 On earth as it is in heaven,
  Hallowèd be Thy name!
  Give us this day our daily bread,
  Hallowèd be Thy name!

3 And forgive us all our debts,
  Hallowèd be Thy name!
  Just as we forgive our debtors,
  Hallowèd be Thy name!

4 Lead us not into temptation,
  Hallowèd be Thy name!
  But deliver us from evil,
  Hallowèd be Thy name!

5 For Thine is the Kingdom and the pow'r and the glory,
  Hallowèd be Thy name!
  For ever and ever, for ever and ever,
  Hallowèd be Thy name!

6 Amen, it shall be so,
  Hallowèd be Thy name!
  Amen, it shall be so,
  Hallowèd be Thy name!
  Hallowèd be Thy name!

Matthew 6: 9–13

118 There is a green hill

1 There is a green hill far away,
Outside a city wall,
Where the dear Lord was crucified
Who died to save us all.

2 We may not know, we cannot tell
What pains He had to bear;
But we believe it was for us
He hung and suffered there.

3 He died that we might be forgiv'n,
He died to make us good,
That we might go at last to heav'n
Saved by His precious blood.

4 There was no other good enough
To pay the price of sin;
He only could unlock the gate
Of heav'n, and let us in.

5 O dearly, dearly has He loved,
And we must love Him too,
And trust in His redeeming blood,
And try His works to do.

Mrs C.F. Alexander (1818–95)

Romans 5: 8

119 There's a time for ev'rything

1 There's a time for ev'rything on earth we're told,
A preacher without hope said this in time of old;
There's time to plant, a time to reap,
Time to throw, a time to keep,
But later hope for life God did unfold.

2 There's a time for ev'rything on earth we're told,
A preacher without hope said this in time of old;
There's time to laugh, a time to cry,
Time to live, a time to die,
But later hope for life God did unfold.

3 There's a time for ev'rything on earth we're told,
A preacher without hope said this in time of old;
There's time to dance, a time to grieve,
Time to take, a time to give,
But later hope for life God did unfold.

4 There's a time for ev'rything on earth we're told,
A preacher without hope said this in time of old;
There's time to lose, a time to find,
Time to loose, a time to bind,
But later hope for life God did unfold.

5 There's a time for ev'rything on earth we're told,
A preacher without hope said this in time of old;
There's time to mend, a time to tear,
Time to hate, a time to care,
But later hope for life God did unfold.

6 There's a time for ev'rything on earth we're told,
A preacher without hope said this in time of old;
There's time for war, a time for peace,
Time to talk, a time to cease,
But later hope for life God did unfold.

7 There's a time for ev'rything on earth we're told,
A preacher without hope said this in time of old;
There's nothing when you come to die,
Live life well, don't pass it by,
But later hope for life God did unfold.

Brenda Irene Piper

Ecclesiastes 3

120 There was a trav'ller

Brenda Irene Piper

Introduction and interlude

Rolling rhythm

There was a trav'-ller, He left a good home,___ He took all his mon-ey to

wan-der and roam; There was a trav'-ller, He left all his own,___ He

left all the love he___ was shown;___ He walked on for miles___ and

went far a-way,___ *Verses 2 and 3* Spend-ing his mon-ey___ day af-ter day;___ *Verses 2 and 3*

There was a trav'-ller, He left a good home___And left all the love he was shown.___

Words and music: © Brenda Irene Piper

138

Suggested ostinato rhythm for percussion:

1 There was a trav'ller,
He left a good home,
He took all his money to wander
    and roam;
There was a trav'ller,
He left all his own,
He left all the love he was shown;
He walked on for miles and went
    far away,
Spending his money day after day;
There was a trav'ller,
He left a good home
And left all the love he was shown.

2 There was a trav'ller,
He spent all he had,
He felt very hungry and then
    he felt sad;
There was a trav'ller,
He knew he'd been bad,
He lost all his friends then felt mad;
He came to his senses and home then
    did run,
To say he was sorry for all he'd done;
His father received him
Back into his home
And said, 'I love you, you're my own.'

3 This trav'ller's brother,
Who stayed home instead,
Had thought of his brother as being long dead;
This trav'ller's brother,
Felt jealousy strong,
His brother had done so much wrong;
But ev'ryone else was filled with delight,
A welcome back party lasted all night;
The father forgave all
His son's sinful past,
With joy he was home now at last.

Brenda Irene Piper

Luke 15: 11–32

121 The Virgin Mary had a baby boy

West Indian carol
melody from the
Edric Connor Collection

Introduction and interlude
Calypso style

The Vir-gin Ma-ry had a baby boy,___ The Vir-gin Ma-ry had a baby boy,___ The Vir-gin Ma-ry had a baby boy,___ And they say that His name was Je-sus.

CHORUS

He come___ from the glo-ry— He come___ from the glo-ri-ous king-dom; He come___ from the glo-ry— He come from the glo-ri-ous king-dom; Oh, yes! be-liev-er, Oh, yes! be-liev-er, He come___ from the glo - ry —   He come— from the glo - ri - ous king - dom.

Suggested ostinato rhythm for Latin American percussion:

1 The Virgin Mary had a baby boy,
   The Virgin Mary had a baby boy,
   The Virgin Mary had a baby boy,
   And they say that His name was Jesus.

   He come from the glory —
   He come from the glorious kingdom;
   He come from the glory —
   He come from the glorious kingdom;
   Oh, yes! believer,
   Oh, yes! believer,
   He come from the glory —
   He come from the glorious kingdom.

2 The angels sang when the baby was born,
   The angels sang when the baby was born,
   The angels sang when the baby was born,
   And proclaimed Him the Saviour Jesus.
        He come from the glory . . .

3 The wise men saw where the baby was born,
   The wise men saw where the baby was born,
   The wise men saw where the baby was born,
   And they saw that His name was Jesus.
        He come from the glory . . .

West Indian carol
from the Edric Connor Collection

Collected and arranged by Edric Connor and Hal Evans.
Copyright © by Boosey & Co. Ltd. 1945. Reproduced by permission of Boosey and Hawkes Music Publishers Ltd.

122 The zither carol

Czech folk dance

VERSE

Girls and boys, leave your toys, make no noise, Kneel at His
crib and wor-ship Him. At Thy shrine, Child Di-vine, we are Thine, Our Sav-iour's
here.

CHORUS

'Hal-le-lu-jah' the church bells ring, 'Hal-le-lu-jah' the

an - gels sing, 'Hal-le - lu - jah' from ev - 'ry-thing. All must draw near.

1 Girls and boys, leave your toys, make no noise,
   Kneel at His crib and worship Him.
   At Thy shrine, Child Divine, we are Thine,
   Our Saviour's here.

   'Hallelujah' the church bells ring,
   'Hallelujah' the angels sing,
   'Hallelujah' from ev'rything.
   All must draw near.

2 On that day, far away, Jesus lay,
   Angels were watching round His head.
   Holy Child, mother mild, undefiled,
   We sing Thy praise.
      'Hallelujah' the church bells . . .

3 Shepherds came at the fame of Thy name,
   Angels their guide to Bethlehem.
   In that place, saw Thy face, filled with grace,
   Stood at Thy door.
      'Hallelujah' the church bells . . .

                                    Sir Malcolm Sargent

123 Thine be the glory

G.F. Handel (1685–1759)

MACCABAEUS

Capo 2(C)

Triumphantly

Thine be the glo - ry, ri - sen, — con-qu'ring Son,

End - less — is the vic - t'ry Thou o'er — death hast won;

An - gels — in bright rai - ment rolled the stone a - way,

Kept — the — fold ed grave-clothes, where Thy — bo - dy lay.

Thine be the glo - ry, ri - sen, — con - qu'ring Son,

End - less — is the vic - t'ry Thou o'er — death hast won.

Suggested ostinato rhythm for percussion:

144

1 Thine be the glory, risen, conqu'ring Son,
  Endless is the vict'ry Thou o'er death hast won;
  Angels in bright raiment rolled the stone away,
  Kept the folded grave-clothes, where Thy body lay.

  Thine be the glory, risen, conqu'ring Son,
  Endless is the vict'ry Thou o'er death hast won.

2 Lo! Jesus meets us, risen from the tomb;
  Lovingly He greets us, scatters fear and gloom;
  Let the Church with gladness hymns of triumph sing,
  For her Lord now liveth; death hath lost its sting.

  Thine be the glory, risen, conqu'ring Son,
  Endless is the vict'ry Thou o'er death hast won.

3 No more we doubt Thee, glorious Prince of life;
  Life is nought without Thee: aid us in our strife;
  Make us more than conqu'rors, through Thy deathless love:
  Bring us safe through Jordan to Thy home above.

  Thine be the glory, risen, conqu'ring Son,
  Endless is the vict'ry Thou o'er death hast won.

Edmond Budry (1854–1932),
trans. R. Birch Hoyle (1875–1939)

124 This is the day

Les Garratt

Brightly with pace

This is the day, This is the day That the Lord has made, That the Lord has made; We shall re-joice, We shall re-joice And be glad in it, And be glad in it. This is the day that the Lord has made, We shall re-joice and be glad in it;

This is the day,
This is the day
That the Lord has made,
That the Lord has made;
We shall rejoice,
We shall rejoice
And be glad in it,
And be glad in it.
This is the day that the Lord has made,
We shall rejoice and be glad in it;
This is the day, this is the day that the Lord has made.

Les Garratt

Psalm 118: 24

125 This joyful Eastertide

1 This joyful Eastertide,
   What need is there for grieving?
   Cast all your care aside
   And be not unbelieving:

   Come, share our Easter joy
   That death could not imprison,
   Nor any pow'r destroy,
   Our Christ, who is arisen,
   Arisen, arisen, arisen!

2 No work for Him is vain,
   No faith in Him mistaken,
   For Easter makes it plain
   His kingdom is not shaken:
   Come, share our Easter . . .

3 Then put your trust in Christ,
   In waking or in sleeping.
   His grace on earth sufficed;
   He'll never quit His keeping:
   Come, share our Easter . . .

Fred Pratt Green

126 Thou didst leave Thy throne

1 Thou didst leave Thy throne
  And Thy kingly crown,
  When Thou camest to earth for me;
  But in Bethlehem's home
  There was found no room
  For Thy holy nativity:
  O come to my heart, Lord Jesus;
  There is room in my heart for Thee.

2 Heaven's arches rang
  When the angels sang,
  Proclaiming Thy royal degree;
  But of lowly birth
  Cam'st Thou, Lord, on earth,
  And in great humility:
  O come to my heart, Lord Jesus;
  There is room in my heart for Thee.

3 The foxes found rest,
  And the birds their nest,
  In the shade of the cedar-tree;
  But Thy couch was the sod,
  O Thou Son of God,
  In the deserts of Galilee:
  O come to my heart, Lord Jesus;
  There is room in my heart for Thee.

4 Thou camest, O Lord,
  With the living word
  That should set Thy people free;
  But, with mocking scorn
  And with crown of thorn,
  They bore Thee to Calvary:
  O come to my heart, Lord Jesus;
  Thy cross is my only plea.

5 When heaven's arches ring,
  And her choirs shall sing,
  At Thy coming to victory,
  Let Thy voice call me home,
  Saying, 'Yet there is room,
  There is room at My side for thee!'
  And my heart shall rejoice, Lord Jesus,
  When Thou comest and callest for me.

Emily Elizabeth Steele Elliott (1836–97)

127 Thou, whose almighty word

1 Thou, whose almighty word
  Chaos and darkness heard,
  And took their flight;
  Hear us, we humbly pray,
  And where the gospel day
  Sheds not its glorious ray,
  Let there be light!

2 Thou, who didst come to bring
  On Thy redeeming wing
  Healing and sight,
  Health to the sick in mind,
  Sight to the inly blind,
  O now to all mankind
  Let there be light!

3 Spirit of truth and love,
  Life-giving, holy Dove,
  Speed forth Thy flight;
  Move on the waters' face,
  Bearing the lamp of grace,
  And in earth's darkest place
  Let there be light!

4 Blessèd and holy Three,
  Glorious Trinity,
  Wisdom, love, might;
  Boundless as ocean's tide
  Rolling in fullest pride,
  Through the world far and wide
  Let there be light!

John Marriott (1780–1825)

128 To God be the glory!

1 To God be the glory! Great things He hath done!
So loved He the world that He gave us His Son;
Who yielded His life an atonement for sin,
And opened the life gate that all may go in.

Praise the Lord! Praise the Lord! Let the earth hear His voice!
Praise the Lord! Praise the Lord! Let the people rejoice!
O come to the Father, through Jesus the Son:
And give Him the glory! Great things He hath done!

2 O perfect redemption, the purchase of blood!
To ev'ry believer the promise of God;
The vilest offender who truly believes,
That moment from Jesus a pardon receives.
    Praise the Lord! . . .

3 Great things He hath taught us, great things He hath done,
And great our rejoicing through Jesus the Son;
But purer, and higher, and greater will be
Our wonder, our rapture, when Jesus we see.
    Praise the Lord! . . .

Frances van Alstyne (1820–1915)

129 Trust in the Lord

Brenda Irene Piper

Capo 5(C)

With emphasis

Trust in the Lord with all your heart, And lean not un-to your own un-der-stand-ing:

In   all your ways   ac-know-ledge Him, And   He shall di-rect your paths.

Tune

Trust in the Lord,   Trust in the Lord, And lean not un-to your own un-der-stand-ing:

Descant

Trust in the Lord,   Trust in the Lord, And   He shall di-rect your   paths.

Trust in the Lord with all your heart,
And lean not unto your own understanding:
In all your ways acknowledge Him,
And He shall direct your paths.
Trust in the Lord,
Trust in the Lord,
And lean not unto your own understanding:
Trust in the Lord,
Trust in the Lord,
And He shall direct your paths.

Brenda Irene Piper

Proverbs 3: 5, 6

130 We are trav'lling

Brenda Irene Piper

Introduction and interlude
Lively and with emphasis

Capo 5(C)

We are trav'-lling a-long life's jour-ney___ And are lost if not in the light; We are trav'-lling a-long life's jour - ney And need to fol-low Christ to be all right. So let us walk in the light, Let us walk in the light; We'll nev - er walk in dark-ness But will have the light of life, If we keep fol-low-ing the world's true light.

Suggested ostinato rhythm for percussion:

154

1 We are trav'lling along life's journey
   And are lost if not in the light;
   We are trav'lling along life's journey
   And need to follow Christ to be all right.

   So let us walk in the light,
   Let us walk in the light;
   We'll never walk in darkness
   But will have the light of life,
   If we keep following the world's true light.

2 If we travel along life's journey
   Without Christ it is always night;
   If we travel along life's journey
   Without the Lord the way will not be right.
      So let us walk . . .

3 As we travel along life's journey
   Let us go only where there's light;
   As we travel along life's journey
   Let's keep the light of the whole world in sight.
      So let us walk . . .

                                          Brenda Irene Piper

John 8: 12

155

131 We can probe amongst the stars

1 We can probe amongst the stars,
   Fathom mysteries with skill,
   People like you and me;
   Yet we watch our brothers starve,
   And we hate and lie and kill;
   People like us need a Saviour.

2 We can harness raging pow'r,
   Build our towers to the sky,
   People like you and me;
   Yet our longings never flow'r,
   And our dreams of glory die;
   People like us need a Saviour.

3 We were made to be God's friends,
   And without Him we are dead,
   People like you and me;
   Jesus' mercy never ends,
   Into life by Him we're led;
   People like us have a Saviour.

Frank Cooke

132 We plough the fields, and scatter

1 We plough the fields, and scatter
The good seed on the land,
But it is fed and watered
By God's almighty hand.
He sends the snow in winter,
The warmth to swell the grain,
The breezes and the sunshine,
And soft refreshing rain:

All good gifts around us
Are sent from heav'n above;
Then thank the Lord, O thank the Lord,
For all His love.

2 He only is the Maker
Of all things near and far;
He paints the wayside flower,
He lights the evening star.
The winds and waves obey Him,
By Him the birds are fed;
Much more to us, His children,
He gives our daily bread:
All good gifts . . .

3 We thank Thee then, O Father,
For all things bright and good;
The seed-time and the harvest,
Our life, our health, our food.
Accept the gifts we offer
For all Thy love imparts,
And, what Thou most desirest,
Our humble, thankful hearts:
All good gifts . . .

M. Claudius (1740–1815),
trans. J.M. Campbell (1817–78)

133 We really want to thank You, Lord

We really want to thank You, Lord.
We really want to bless Your name.
Hallelujah! Jesus is our King!

We really want to thank You, Lord.
We really want to bless Your name.
Hallelujah! Jesus is our King!

1 We thank You, Lord, for Your gift to us,
   Your life so rich beyond compare,
   The gift of Your body here on earth
   Of which we sing and share.
       We really want to thank . . .

2 We thank You, Lord, for our life together,
   To live and move in the love of Christ,
   Your tenderness which sets us free
   To serve You with our lives.
       We really want to thank . . .

3 Praise God from whom all blessings flow,
   Praise Him all creatures here below.
   Praise Him above you heavenly host,
   Praise Father, Son and Holy Ghost.
       We really want to thank . . .

Ed Baggett

134 We three kings of Orient are

1 We three kings of Orient are;
Bearing gifts we traverse afar
Field and fountain, moor and mountain,
Following yonder star:

O star of wonder, star of night,
Star with royal beauty bright,
Westward leading, still proceeding,
Guide us to thy perfect light.

2 Born a King on Bethlehem plain,
Gold I bring, to crown Him again –
King for ever, ceasing never
Over us all to reign:
O star of wonder . . .

3 Frankincense to offer have I;
Incense owns a Deity nigh:
Prayer and praising, all men raising,
Worship Him, God most high:
O star of wonder . . .

4 Myrrh is mine; its bitter perfume
Breathes a life of gathering gloom;
Sorrowing, sighing, bleeding, dying,
Sealed in the stone-cold tomb:
O star of wonder . . .

5 Glorious now behold Him arise,
King, and God, and sacrifice!
Heav'n sings alleluya,
Alleluya the earth replies:
O star of wonder . . .

J.H. Hopkins, Jnr. (1820–91)

135 We've a story to tell to the nations

H. Ernest Nichol
(1862–1926)
Capo 2(C)

MESSAGE

With boldness

Suggested accompaniment:
brass and drums

160

1 We've a story to tell to the nations,
That shall turn their hearts to the right;
A story of truth and mercy,
A story of peace and light, a story of peace and light.

For the darkness shall turn to dawning,
And the dawning to noon-day bright,
And Christ's great kingdom shall come on earth,
The kingdom of love and light.

2 We've a song to be sung to the nations,
That shall lift their hearts to the Lord;
A song that shall conquer evil,
And shatter the spear and sword, and shatter the spear and sword.
For the darkness . . .

3 We've a message to give to the nations,
That the Lord who's reigning above
Has sent us His Son to save us,
And show us that God is love, and show us that God is love.
For the darkness . . .

4 We've a Saviour to show to the nations,
Who the path of sorrow has trod,
That all of the whole world's people
Might come to the truth of God, might come to the truth of God.
For the darkness . . .

Colin Sterne (1862–1926) altered

136 *What a friend we have in Jesus*

C.C. Converse (1832–1918)

CONVERSE

Capo 1(E)

Tune: What a friend we have in Je - sus, All our sins and griefs to

Descant: What a friend we have in Je - sus,

bear! What a priv - i - lege to car - ry

All our sins and griefs to bear! What a priv - i - lege to

Ev - 'ry-thing to God in prayer! O what peace we oft - en

car - ry Ev - 'ry-thing to God in prayer!

for - feit, O what need-less pain we bear,

O what peace we oft-en for - feit, O what need-less pain we

All be-cause we do not car - ry Ev - 'ry-thing to God in prayer!

bear, All be-cause we do not car-ry Ev-'ry-thing to God in prayer!

1 What a friend we have in Jesus,
All our sins and griefs to bear!
What a privilege to carry
Ev'rything to God in prayer!
O what peace we often forfeit,
O what needless pain we bear,
All because we do not carry
Ev'rything to God in prayer!

2 Have we trials and temptations?
Is there trouble anywhere?
We should never be discouraged,
Take it to the Lord in prayer!
Can we find a friend so faithful
Who will all our sorrows share?
Jesus knows our ev'ry weakness,
Take it to the Lord in prayer!

3 Are we weak and heavy-laden,
Cumbered with a load of care?
Jesus only is our refuge,
Take it to the Lord in prayer!
Do thy friends despise, forsake thee?
Take it to the Lord in prayer!
In His arms He'll take and shield thee,
Thou wilt find a solace there.

Joseph Scriven (1819–86)

137 What a wonderful Saviour is Jesus!

composer unknown

Joyfully

VERSE

What a won-der-ful Sav-iour is Je-sus!___ What a won-der-ful friend is He; For He left all the glo-ry of hea-ven,___ Came to earth to die on Cal-va-ry:

CHORUS

Tune

Sing ho-san-na, sing ho-san-na, Sing ho-san-na to the King of Kings!

Descant

Sing,___ Sing,___ Sing,___ Sing, Sing, Sing!

Sing ho-san-na, sing ho-san-na, Sing ho-san-na to the King!

Sing,___ Sing,___ Sing,___ Sing!___

1 What a wonderful Saviour is Jesus!
  What a wonderful friend is He;
  For He left all the glory of heaven,
  Came to earth to die on Calvary:

  Sing hosanna, sing hosanna,
  Sing hosanna to the King of Kings!
  Sing hosanna, sing hosanna,
  Sing hosanna to the King!

2 He arose from the grave – alleluia!
  And He lives never more to die;
  At the Father's right hand interceding,
  He will hear and heed our faintest cry:
    Sing hosanna . . .

3 He is coming some day to receive us –
  We'll be caught up to heav'n above;
  What a joy it will be to behold Him –
  Sing forever of His grace and love!
    Sing hosanna . . .

  author unknown

138 When morning gilds the skies

1 When morning gilds the skies,
My heart awaking cries:
May Jesus Christ be praised!
Alike at work and prayer
To Jesus I repair:
May Jesus Christ be praised!

2 Does sadness fill my mind?
A solace here I find:
May Jesus Christ be praised!
When evil thoughts molest,
With this I shield my breast:
May Jesus Christ be praised!

3 Be this, when day is past
Of all my thoughts the last:
May Jesus Christ be praised!
The night becomes as day,
When from the heart we say:
May Jesus Christ be praised!

4 To God, the Word, on high
The hosts of angels cry:
May Jesus Christ be praised!
Let mortals, too, upraise
Their voice in hymns of praise:
May Jesus Christ be praised!

5 Let earth's wide circle round
   In joyful notes resound:
   May Jesus Christ be praised!
   Let air, and sea, and sky,
   From depth to height, reply:
   May Jesus Christ be praised!

6 Be this while life is mine,
   My canticle divine:
   May Jesus Christ be praised!
   Be this the eternal song
   Through all the ages long:
   May Jesus Christ be praised!

anonymous,
trans. Edward Caswall (1814–78)

139 When we talk there's always someone

Brenda Irene Piper

Introduction

With expression

VERSE

When we talk there's al - ways some - one Who will hear the words we say; When we walk there's al - ways some - one Who will watch us all the way; We nev - er need be wor - ried Or fright-ened a - ny-where, For God loves ev-'ry-one of us And He is al-ways there.

CHORUS

I will talk — Talk to God, As He is list' - ning for me; I will talk — Talk to God, For I want Him my___ friend to be.

Fine Interlude *D.S.*

Suggested accompaniment during chorus: violins

168

1 When we talk there's always someone
  Who will hear the words we say;
  When we walk there's always someone
  Who will watch us all the way;
  We never need be worried
  Or frightened anywhere,
  For God loves ev'ryone of us
  And He is always there.

  I will talk –
  Talk to God,
  As He is list'ning for me;
  I will talk –
  Talk to God,
  For I want Him my friend to be.

2 When we call there's always someone
  Who will come and with us dine;
  When we fall there's always someone
  Who will reach your hand and mine;
  We never need feel lonely
  Or wonder who will care,
  For God loves ev'ryone of us
  And He is always there.
    I will talk . . .

3 When we cry there's always someone
  Who will feel our ev'ry pain;
  When we die there's always someone
  Who can make us rise again;
  Our hearts need not feel heavy,
  But lightened when we share,
  For God loves ev'ryone of us
  And He is always there.
    I will talk . . .

Brenda Irene Piper

140 *When we walk with the Lord*

1 When we walk with the Lord
In the light of His Word
What a glory He sheds on our way!
While we do His good will,
He abides with us still,
And with all who will trust and obey.

Trust and obey, for there's no other way
To be happy in Jesus,
But to trust and obey.

2 Not a shadow can rise,
Not a cloud in the skies,
But His smile quickly drives it away;
Not a doubt nor a fear,
Not a sigh nor a tear,
Can abide while we trust and obey.
   Trust and obey . . .

3 Not a burden we bear,
Not a sorrow we share,
But our toil He doth richly repay;
Not a grief nor a loss,
Not a frown nor a cross,
But is blest if we trust and obey.
   Trust and obey . . .

4 But we never can prove
The delights of His love
Until all on the altar we lay;
For the favour He shows,
And the joy He bestows,
Are for those who will trust and obey.
   Trust and obey . . .

5 Then in fellowship sweet
We will sit at His feet,
Or we'll walk by His side in the way;
What He says we will do,
Where He sends we will go –
Never fear, only trust and obey.
   Trust and obey . . .

John Henry Sammis (1846–1919)

141 When I survey the wondrous cross

1 When I survey the wondrous cross
   On which the Prince of glory died,
   My richest gain I count but loss,
   And pour contempt on all my pride.

2 Forbid it, Lord, that I should boast,
   Save in the death of Christ my God:
   All the vain things that charm me most,
   I sacrifice them to His blood.

3 See from His head, His hands, His feet,
   Sorrow and love flow mingled down:
   Did e'er such love and sorrow meet,
   Or thorns compose so rich a crown?

4 Were the whole realm of nature mine,
   That were an off'ring far too small,
   Love so amazing, so divine,
   Demands my soul, my life, my all.

Isaac Watts (1674–1748)

142 While shepherds watched

1 While shepherds watched their flocks by night,
All seated on the ground,
The angel of the Lord came down,
And glory shone around.

2 'Fear not,' said he (for mighty dread
Had seized their troubled mind);
'Glad tidings of great joy I bring
To you and all mankind.'

3 'To you in David's town this day
Is born of David's line
A Saviour, who is Christ the Lord;
And this shall be the sign:

4 'The heav'nly Babe you there shall find
To human view displayed,
All meanly wrapped in swaddling bands,
And in a manger laid.'

5 Thus spake the seraph: and forthwith
Appeared a shining throng
Of angels praising God, who thus
Addressed their joyful song:

6 'All glory be to God on high,
And to the earth be peace;
Good-will henceforth from heav'n to men
Begin and never cease.'

Nahum Tate (1652–1715)

143 Who is He in yonder stall

1 Who is He in yonder stall,
At whose feet the shepherds fall?

'Tis the Lord! O wondrous story!
'Tis the Lord, the King of glory!
At His feet we humbly fall;
Crown Him! Crown Him, Lord of all!

2 Who is He to whom they bring
All the sick and sorrowing?
'Tis the Lord! . . .

3 Who is He that stands and weeps
At the grave where Lazarus sleeps?
'Tis the Lord! . . .

4 Who is He on yonder tree
Dies in pain and agony?
'Tis the Lord! . . .

5 Who is He who from the grave
Comes to rescue, help and save?
'Tis the Lord! . . .

6 Who is He who from His throne
Sends the Spirit to His own?
'Tis the Lord! . . .

7 Who is He who comes again,
Judge of angels and of men?
'Tis the Lord! . . .

Benjamin Russell Hanby (1833–67), altered

144 Yesterday, today, for ever

composer unknown

Yes - ter - day, _ to - day, for ev - er, Je - sus is ___ the same;

All may change, but Je - sus nev - er, Glo - ry to His Name!

Glo - ry to His Name! Glo - ry to ___ His Name!

All may change, but Je - sus nev - er, Glo - ry to His Name!

Yesterday, today, for ever,
Jesus is the same;
All may change, but Jesus never,
Glory to His Name! *(3 times)*

All may change, but Jesus never,
Glory to His Name!

author unknown

Chime bars part: © Brenda Irene Piper

Hebrews 13: 8